Motherhood After 35

Motherhood After 35

Choices, Decisions, Options

Maggie Jones

FISHER
er
BOOKS™

Publishers: Bill Fisher
            Helen V. Fisher
            Howard W. Fisher
Managing editor: Sarah Trotta
Book design: Deanie Wood
Cover design
& production: Randy Schultz
               Deanie Wood

Published by Fisher Books
4239 W. Ina Road, Suite 101
Tucson, Arizona 85741
(520) 744-6110

Printed in U.S.A.
10 9 8 7 6 5 4 3 2 1

**Library of Congress
Cataloging-in Publication Data**

Jones, Maggie.
  [Choosing older motherhood]
  Motherhood After 35: choices,
decisions, options / Maggie Jones.
      p. cm.
  British ed. published in 1996
under title: Choosing older
motherhood.
  Includes bibliographical
references and index.
  ISBN 1-55561-149-4
  1. Pregnancy in middle age--
United States. 2. Childbirth in
middle age--United States.
3. Middle aged women--United
States--Psychology. I. Title.
RG556.6.J66 1998
618.2--dc21   98-12305
                     CIP

First published in the United Kingdom by Vermilion in 1996

Contents

About the Author

Maggie Jones is a freelance journalist and the author of 11 books on health and childcare issues. She is also a breastfeeding counselor. Ms. Jones is married and has three children.

Foreword

How refreshing it is to find a book specifically focused on older-age parenthood! Modern society has become so mesmerized into thinking that those wishing to have a family over the age of 40 are somehow selfish and their children will inevitably be disadvantaged emotionally and in other ways. Informative and sensible literature on this subject has been largely lacking.

Our present society has a short memory: Natural fertility *does* normally occur beyond age 40, even allowing for the fact there is an increased incidence of chromosomal abnormalities and miscarriage. But we are now less aware of older-age couples having children simply because many fertile women who would previously have had large families into their late forties can elect not to.

However, for those having their first child at this time, whether from natural fertility or as a result of assisted conception, pregnancy does present an uncharted course full of anxieties and expectations, which appear to be disproportionately exaggerated by the reaction of the public and even some members of the medical profession.

Maggie Jones's book has much to recommend it. It is easy to read, without technical jargon. Its logical layout starts from the decision-making process for pregnancy at an older age, and then sensibly draws attention to the increased difficulty of becoming parents with conventional and even assisted-conception treatment, including IVF and other related methods. Even so, Ms. Jones correctly indicates that the availability of egg donation has transformed the prospects of success of fertility treatment: Having a family is now more, rather than less, likely for those fortunate enough to be able to receive this method of treatment.

Her descriptive explanations of what to expect when pregnancy does result, of prenatal screening and the birth itself, are liberally interspersed with quotes from real couples. These couples express both negative and positive reactions about different experiences, even when they are rightly or wrongly critical of the medical profession. Their responses indicate the author's commitment to telling the whole story, in the process allowing the reader to identify with how she would react in similar circumstances.

I recommend this book to those who hope to experience one of life's recurring marvels—the generation and birth of a new being to a couple who, despite some anxiety about becoming parents at an older age, wishes to share the overwhelming joy of becoming a family.

Ian Craft, M.D.
Fellow of the Royal College of Surgeons
Fellow of the Royal College of Obstetricians
  and Gynecologists

Introduction

More and more women today are choosing to have their babies later in life – that is, in their thirties and early forties. Statistics from the March of Dimes Perinatal Data Center show that, yes, later motherhood is on the increase. Most of the births occurring each year are to women in their mid- to late twenties. But the proportion of births to women 35 years and older has increased by 84% between 1983 and 1993, from 5.7% of births to 10.5%. In 1976, 19 of 1,000 U.S. births were to women between 35 and 39 years old. By 1996, births to women in this age group accounted for 35.4 of 1,000 births. Women over 40 accounted for 4.5 births per 1,000 in 1976. By 1996, women between 40 and 44 accounted for 6.8 births per 1,000.

Between 1980 and 1990 the number of births outside marriage to women over 30 tripled. It is estimated that about three-quarters of these births were to divorced or separated women. Many of these women were living with their new partners.

While most women who delay motherhood choose to have children in their late thirties, a few decide to become mothers for the first time in their forties. More and more women are establishing their careers first and then embarking on motherhood. Recently, many career women have embarked on motherhood later in their lives, presenting an image of the youthful, sexy, attractive older mother. You may know some of them yourself! Actresses Jane Seymour and Priscilla Presley are two well-known examples of women who have given birth to children in their forties.

Many pregnancies to older women are still accidental, as is shown by the number of women over 40 who choose to terminate their pregnancies. In 1988, 109,642 U.S. women over 40 were pregnant. Of these, 44% chose to terminate the pregnancy. Fifty-six percent chose to give birth. (Alan Guttmacher Institute, *Facts in Brief*; January 4, 1993)

Although menopause in most women occurs sometime between the age of 45 and 55, most women trying to have a baby in their forties do experience fertility problems. Now new infertility treatment has given hope to older women unable to conceive naturally. The news in 1997 that a 63-year-old American woman had conceived was greeted with some controversy and confusion. Public debate centered on whether it was "right" for a woman who could be a grandmother to give birth and whether she would be an adequate mother for her children, not to mention whether it was moral for doctors to use artificial means to induce a pregnancy in women over the natural age of child rearing. (In fairness to the doctors, she had told them she was years younger.) But what is the "natural" age at which fertility ends? The oldest mother on record to have conceived naturally appears to be Mrs. Ruth Kistler of Los Angeles, who gave birth to her daughter at the age of 57 years, 129 days.

The reduction in the numbers of women who have very late babies has probably changed people's attitudes so that today it seems more "unnatural" for women to have a very late baby than it seemed to earlier generations. For women to have a late baby by accident seems to require help and sympathy, while to choose to have a baby late—perhaps with help from medical science—seems to inspire judgmental attitudes. Late motherhood is seen as an indulgence in a generation of women who want to "have it all;" it is not meant to be good for the baby.

Everyone seems to accept that late motherhood carries some risk—for the woman's health, the baby's health, and perhaps their happiness later on. But what are the risks of late motherhood? What chances is the older mother taking with her health and life? What are the chances of her succeeding in having a healthy pregnancy and normal labor? What are the actual risks of having a baby with disabilities? And how successful is parenthood for the older mother, her family, and, especially, for the child? This book will try to answer these questions for those of you who are considering having a baby later in life.

$\sim$ 1 $\sim$

Making the Decision

Women have more freedom today to plan when to have a family than ever before. Contraception and legal termination of pregnancy are freely available. At least in theory, most women don't have to have children until they are ready.

Many women today expect to find fulfillment not only as a wife and mother but also through a career. The number of women in full-time employment continues to increase, and many women can choose to have babies knowing their job will be waiting for them on their return. More and more women are choosing to postpone having their first child until a baby fits in with their lives, marriages and careers.

⌐ Having a baby at this time

Most of us believe having a baby is the result of a rational decision, but interviews with older mothers show this is actually far from the truth. Careless use of contraception, a decision made suddenly because a sister or best friend has a baby, boredom or lack of satisfaction with a job, doubts about one's fertility and fear that "time is running out" and the choice may be taken away are more common answers to the question, "What made you decide to have a baby?" than "We felt it was the right time." Perhaps such reasons are more common among late mothers; perhaps more women who "choose" to have their families would decide to have two children, two or three years apart, in their late 20s or early 30s.

Still, most women probably do not "plan" their families in the usual sense. Many women are ambivalent about whether or when to have a child; a wanted pregnancy can finish as a termination, especially when a partner rejects the idea of a baby or the woman's circumstances change. Just as often, an unwelcome pregnancy can become a much-loved child. All contraceptive methods have a failure rate, especially when used for ten years or more. Women's doubts about their fertility, especially as they grow older, may lead them to "take risks" to see whether they can conceive. Many women find it takes them longer to conceive than they expected (the average is 6 months). Others experience problems with their fertility or have miscarriages.

Little research is available on the reasons women have children late. One study, carried out by Kate Windridge and Judy Berryman at Leicester University in England, looked at 346 women who had babies at the age of 40 or later. One hundred were first-time mothers. They were not representative of the general population—they had responded to advertisements in women's magazines and periodicals, and were mostly in professional occupations—but the findings are still interesting. Only 5% said they had delayed having their babies for career reasons. Less than half of the babies were planned. Forty percent of the first-time mothers over 40 had sought advice on fertility problems, so infertility may have been responsible at least in part for a delay in becoming a mother.

Many women are ambivalent about whether or when to have a child.

For some women, the decision is uncomplicated. "I had always thought that my mid-thirties was about the right time to have children," says Jenny. "It gave us five years to enjoy being a couple, having adventurous vacations and all that, and also earning enough to get the house the way we wanted it. I was a little worried about my fertility declining, so I didn't want to leave it later than 35. It took me four months to get pregnant, I took maternity leave, and then I had my second child two years later. I'm still working part-time, and I have a great place for day care. Everything's worked out really well for us."

For many women, however, reality doesn't work out as smoothly as this. Susie had her first baby at 38 and her second at 42. "A friend of mine, a doctor, got married at 34, decided to start a family two years later at the same time as me. She wanted the babies to be born in the spring. Needless to say, she got pregnant immediately, had a boy in April, and two years later, a girl in May. I just can't stand it! It took me nearly two years to get pregnant at all. Then I had a miscarriage. I had my first child, but then I had two more miscarriages before having my second child four years later. It was very frustrating. I thought I could plan everything, but sometimes you just can't. There's so much talk about choice these days. Little do we know! Nature has a way of getting her revenge sometimes."

Even if women feel they do have a choice, however, making the choice is not always easy. Some women postpone having a baby from year to year, looking forward to a perfect time for bringing a child into the world. "When I

Some women postpone having a baby from year to year, looking forward to a perfect time for bringing a child into the world.

have that promotion . . . when we've moved to a bigger house . . . once we have saved some money. . . ." Postponement can become a way of life. It is easy to put off the childbearing decision year after year—until suddenly there seems to be no time left.

This is what happened to Tina, now age 41. "At first I was enjoying my job so much I didn't want to take a break to have a baby. I was working as a reporter and there were lots of exciting opportunities for me; I worked late a lot, and I knew if I had a child I wouldn't be able to concentrate on my job in the same way.

"Then we decided to move to a bigger house, which needed a lot of work. That went on for two years. Just when we felt we were getting caught up with that, I got a job in Madison and we moved again. By now having a child seemed like a major upheaval and I didn't want to face it. I saw friends of mine becoming nonpeople, talking about nothing but diapers and sleeplessness. I didn't want the same thing to happen to me.

"Now I'm not sure I'll ever have a baby. I haven't used contraception for six months, but nothing's happened. Maybe it's too late. But on the other hand, part of me is relieved not to be pregnant. I wouldn't go rushing to an infertility clinic if nothing happens. But if I do get pregnant, I'll give it a whirl."

Melanie also had doubts about having a child, although she decided to go ahead before it was "too late." "I made a conscious decision to have a baby, a decision I had put off for many years. I was 38 when we started trying, it took four months to conceive, and I was just 39 when our daughter was born.

"When we got married ten years ago we always thought we'd have kids. Alan wanted them more than I did, but he left the decision to me because he knew I would do the majority of everything and that my life would be most changed. I wasn't too into it—I didn't think I'd make a particularly wonderful mother. My own childhood wasn't happy. I had an older brother who bossed me around, and I didn't feel I had any support from my parents.

"*I* didn't suddenly feel I wanted a baby, but I thought if I left it any later I'd regret it."

"I think we realized as I got into my late thirties that it was getting a little late for having a baby. I didn't suddenly feel I wanted a baby, but I thought if I left it any later I'd regret it. I also thought of Alan—having a baby is a natural, normal thing to do. I didn't want to deprive him of that. People kept telling me having a baby was just the greatest thing. I thought I'd probably feel that way too if I did it. After all, we're programmed that way."

Couples who get married young may postpone having children because they feel too immature to cope with the demands children will make. Says one woman, "I think we both felt we needed time together as a couple, to mature, to get to know one another. Then that got to be our state of mind. We wanted to put ourselves and our marriage first. Children were a threat. We kept thinking, will having children spoil our relationship? Will we be driven apart by parenthood?"

Alison recalls that for many years the idea of having a child was too constricting. "We were both having a good time in our careers. Children would have been in the way. There were times when he wanted a child and I said, 'No, not yet,' and times when I suggested it and he said, 'Maybe next year.' We were never sure we wanted children at the same time until it became necessary to have them because I was getting older. I was scared of the responsibility."

For those who have been married for some time, having a baby later means disrupting a familiar life routine and creating upheaval in a long-established relationship. As they watch their friends and colleagues having children and see the disruption, exhaustion and lack of money in their lives, it seems harder and harder to make the decision. "I wanted to have a baby, but frankly I was terrified. When I woke up on Sundays to a leisurely morning of reading the newspaper and then visiting a museum in the afternoon, I kept thinking this wouldn't be possible with kids. I kept thinking, do I really want it? And I really didn't know."

⌒ New interest in children

Some women find the desire for parenthood creeping up on them unawares. Kendra, 38 when she had her first child, described her feelings like this: "I was watching other people with babies or young children with great curiosity, thinking, 'So that's what they do at that age,' 'That woman is breast-feeding,' or 'I don't think that was a good way to handle that situation. I would have done it differently.' I really realized what was happening when I started looking at baby clothes in local stores and reading magazine articles about natural childbirth—with avid interest!"

For others, it's a realization that career and home is not enough. "I'd been working at the company for 16 years. I'd really done well and enjoyed it, but suddenly I felt I was seeing the same thing over and over. Younger people would come in, bursting with ideas, and I'd say, 'Oh, we did that seven years ago, so-and-so did it, try something new.' But for them, and for a lot of other people, it *was* new. It was beginning to get repetitious. I was getting stale; I just couldn't summon the enthusiasm I used to have. I wanted something totally different, a new challenge. That's what motherhood meant."

Many women find themselves unable to make a positive decision to have children, but they may make a more passive one. After all, to prevent pregnancy most women have to take the active step of using contraception. CeCe, at 37, made the decision with her partner to stop taking the Pill. "I'd been taking it long enough and I wanted a change. I was fitted with a cap, and I used that religiously for about two years. Then I really got bored with it. I felt I'd been messing around with contraception all these years, first with an IUD, then the Pill, then the cap. I'd had enough of it. We started getting careless and taking risks. Then one day I got pregnant. I didn't know how I'd react, but I was pleased—I thought, 'I can do it after all.' I felt different, very grown up somehow."

⌒ Circumstances may delay parenthood

While many women do "choose" to have a baby later in life, for many, circumstances dictate when they have a baby. Hope had a first child at 39 because she didn't meet her husband until she was 37. "I had several relationships, but none of them were right. The first man I lived with said he didn't want to have children, ever. With the second man the relationship didn't work out and then I had a long period in which I had a passionate relationship with a man who was totally unreliable. We never lived together; a child would have been out of the question. When I met Marty I knew right away this was it. We were both eager to have children. I got pregnant just before we got married last year."

"*Not finding the right person*" *is a common cause of delayed parenthood.*

Denise was 41 when she conceived her first child. "It wasn't as simple as just career reasons, although that was part of it. My first marriage broke up partly as a result of my career—I was more successful than he was. My career took me overseas as a banking executive . . . For some years I wasn't in a relationship where I could have a child. Then I remarried in 1991 and we both wanted children."

"Not finding the right person" is a common cause of delayed parenthood. Some women go through the agonizing process of wondering whether to get pregnant anyway and become a single mother by choice. "When year after year went by and I didn't get married, I did seriously think about having a baby on my own," says Debbie, now 40. "It was very tempting but I kept wondering if it would be fair to my child. When I met Stephen I remember thinking maybe I should just be careless with contraception and see what happens. But then he said he would like to have a baby with me before I said it."

Disagreements between couples over when to have a baby can be deeply divisive. Often the woman postpones parenthood for years until her partner feels ready. Sometimes he never does. This happened to Ginny. "He said at the beginning that he didn't really want children. I accepted that at first. Then I thought he would probably change his mind as time went by, but he didn't. It's too bad I made such an issue out of it and talked about it so much. It meant I couldn't get pregnant by accident. It would have been obvious to him it was a conscious decision. He was always very careful about contraception. I couldn't have fooled him.

"When I hit 40, things changed all of a sudden. I hated him and hated myself for letting him make the decision for me. I should have said, 'Having a baby is too important for me. If you won't agree, then I'll leave you.' If I had issued an ultimatum he might have changed his mind. I think if we'd actually had a baby, he would have liked it and been a good father. I've seen other men not wild about having a baby turn into doting fathers when the child actually arrives. Now it's too late. I cry all the time because I realize I'll never be a mother. It's driving us apart. In the end I may end up with neither husband nor child."

When the woman postpones childbearing for her partner, the consequences can be even more painful. Ellen went along with her partner's wishes not to have a child. She was enjoying her job and thought he would probably come around. "But then I felt the biological clock ticking and I thought, it's now or never. I told him I wanted to have a child and he said he didn't feel ready. I said, 'Then it will be too late for me.'

"My fortieth birthday came and went and then the bombshell was dropped. He said he had had an affair with his secretary and had made her pregnant. Her family was Catholic and they were going to make her have the baby. He said he had agreed to pay child support but the affair was over and he didn't want to see the mother again. He told me he was deeply ashamed.

"I forgave him and we stayed together. But he does keep in touch with the mother and he does visit his little daughter. Can you imagine how that makes me feel? The other day we were out shopping. I saw him looking at some little girls' shoes in a window. I know he was wondering whether to get them for her. It cut like a knife; I think of that little girl all the time. It torments me, especially at night. He says now that he'd be prepared for me to have a child but I'm 42 and nothing is happening. I should have trusted my instincts and not listened to him."

Some women go ahead and have a baby despite their partner's opposition, either by an accidental pregnancy or by "tricking him into it." Sometimes everything works out well; other times it doesn't. Greg expressed his resistance to having children over many years until his wife became pregnant through a genuine accident: "She'd used the cap for more than ten years. I guess in all that time the chances of something going wrong must be pretty high." The couple discussed having an abortion and Greg agreed that if his wife wanted a baby it would be cruel for him to insist. She had the baby but throughout the pregnancy he remained cool and uninvolved. After the baby was born Greg retreated more and more into his job, until he finally left her altogether.

◡ Not having children

For all those who have delayed parenthood comes a moment of truth, a realization they have not made the decision to have a child and will therefore remain childless. Candace is 43. She says the timing has never been quite right for her to have a baby, although she has not ruled out the possibility altogether. "You have to be a realist and not a romantic about children. It's easy to fantasize about having a baby . . . I'm not sure it's right for me at the moment."

The woman who at 43 has still not decided to have a baby will probably join the increasing numbers of women who are choosing never to have children. Recent statistics have shown a definite increase in the number of women choosing to remain childless. In 1982, 4.9% of all women of childbearing age were voluntarily childless. By 1995, the percentage had increased to 6.6%. (National Center for Health Statistics, 1995) Although there is a shift towards later childbearing, statistics show that this increase in childlessness is likely to continue among younger women.

Aside from those who decide not to have children, there are those who want children very much and are unable to have them. Tremendous advances have been made in infertility treatment over the past two decades. Of the nearly 5 million American couples who report difficulty or delays in achieving a live birth, 1.3 million will receive medical advice or treatment for infertility. According to the *American Medical Association Encyclopedia of Medicine* (1989), professional treatment aids approximately half the women who seek help for fertility problems.

Many women find infertility is a terrible irony after years of using contraception.

For those who have, for whatever reason, postponed having a baby into their mid- to late 30s, infertility can be a devastating blow. "I know it's covered in the papers and I knew it was a risk, but I still didn't think it would ever happen to me," says Gina, 37. "After six months of trying I went to the doctor and he said, 'Give it time. You're not as fertile as you were. If you haven't conceived in another six months we'll do something.' I hadn't, so back to the doctor. He referred us to a clinic, but the first available appointment was three months away. Meanwhile, nothing happened. We had tests. They went on for months; each test had to be done only at the most fertile time of the month, so that took months to arrange. In the end they discovered I had blocked tubes, probably as a result of an appendicitis operation I had when I was a teenager. The discovery that there really was something wrong was appalling. I felt I only had about three years left." Gina conceived two years later on her second attempt at IVF (in-vitro fertilization).

Many women find infertility is a terrible irony after years of using contraception. "I was on the Pill for 12 years. Then I discovered I had never ovulated to begin with. Those pregnancy scares I had when I'd taken chances before I went on the Pill, all those years of swallowing hormones—it all seemed so pointless. I was really angry and distressed."

Rachel had always wanted children, but didn't marry until she was 36. "We tried for a baby immediately. Nothing happened. After about nine months we started to do temperature charts. They seemed to show I was ovulating, and so then there was the awful business of trying to time sex for the most fertile time in my cycle. Those temperature charts started to dominate our sex life— Paul said he couldn't stand being told when to perform. He thought I was being neurotic. Once he found out it wasn't his sperm that were at fault, he lost interest in the whole process. I was devastated—if I didn't have children, what else was there to look forward to?"

Those who remain childless, whether by choice or not, often find themselves put under considerable pressure by others.

Those who remain childless, whether by choice or not, often find themselves put under considerable pressure by others. Questions such as, "So, when are you going to have a baby?" or "Don't you think it's selfish not to have children?" are heard frequently. Some women do feel pressured into having a child by the outside world. "I had been putting it off and putting it off, and I'm not sure I really wanted a child. But then I thought, this is something almost everybody does. Will I feel I've missed something?" Pressure is put on women to have children by family and friends and, notoriously, by parents wanting grandchildren.

"My mother went on and on about having a grandchild and finally I said, 'My career is important to me. If I have a baby, will you take care of it while I go back to work?' She agreed—and it has worked out really well for us." Others are not so lucky or do not give in to parental pressures. This can create a lot of stress in family relationships. "My mother complained about it so much, how unhappy I was making her, that she couldn't see the point in life if she didn't have grandchildren, that I started avoiding her.

Not only does she not have a grandchild, she's on the way to losing her daughter, too."

⌒ Unexpected pregnancy

But, again, the choice to remain childless sometimes comes unstuck with a late and unexpected pregnancy. Then the woman has to make an often painful choice—to have a baby or an abortion. "I was 40. We'd been married three years and agreed that children weren't in the cards. It was a big shock when I got pregnant. My husband said, 'Well, why don't you just have the baby? It might be nice to have one.' I said, 'That's easy for you to say! You don't have to go through pregnancy and birth and everything. If *you* change your mind, you can walk away.' Still, it didn't seem right to have an abortion. I kept thinking this could be the only chance I'd ever have to have a baby. What if I had an abortion and then changed my mind? I'd never be able to live with myself if I thought I'd thrown away my one chance."

The much-older mother may not even be aware she has conceived.

"Getting pregnant made me realize how ambivalent my feelings were about this whole motherhood thing," recalls Gail, who had her first and only baby at 41. "I'd been perfectly happy not to have a child. When I thought I might be pregnant I felt awful—worried and confused. But then, when I got the pregnancy-test result, I was ecstatic! I don't think I'd ever felt that happy. I was so excited and I felt—I know it sounds awful—I felt so womanly, somehow."

For the woman who is much older, pregnancy can seem too remote to be something to count on. "When I remarried in my early 40s, I thought we wouldn't have a child," says Ann, who had three children from her former marriage, then almost grown up. "I did think it would be too bad if John, who was 12 years younger than I, couldn't have a child because of my age. I had a miscarriage when I was 44. That was sad, a disappointment, because I thought it would be my last chance, but it wasn't a great trauma for me.

"I went back to teaching. I didn't take any precautions and I didn't conceive. Then, two years later, my period was late and I felt terrible. When the pregnancy test came back positive I was thrilled, but I'd had two miscarriages and I didn't want to get too excited." A healthy son was born when she was 47.

Heather, who remarried in her mid-thirties, also had miscarriages. "I thought it was too late and I probably wouldn't be able to have a baby. I thought it was too much trouble anyway and I wasn't sure I wanted to try again. The doctors said to wait before I tried again, so I asked Stephen to use a condom. He was careless about it and I conceived, so Margaret is an accident after three miscarriages!"

The much-older mother may not even be aware she has conceived. Marilyn was 43 with two grown-up sons when her periods became somewhat irregular. "I put down the lack of periods to my age, and since I'd always gained weight easily, I didn't really notice what was happening. When I finally went to the doctor and had a pregnancy test I discovered that I was already 20 weeks pregnant. It was really too late to have an abortion."

Accidental pregnancies later in life can cause women—and their partners—to do a lot of soul-searching. "I was 45 when I discovered I was pregnant. I'd become a little careless about contraception. I just didn't think I was fertile any more. At first I thought I'd terminate the pregnancy, and that's what I told my doctor. But then one night I just said to my husband, 'What if I *did* have the baby?' We talked about it and decided to go ahead. We loved one another, we could cope with a baby, and I still feel deep down that ending a pregnancy would be wrong. At the same time, I could have had an abortion, and I have a lot of sympathy for any woman who finds herself having to make that difficult choice. If Len had said no, it would have been very different. There's no way I would have had the baby without his support."

✑ Second time around

Another reason for the increase in births to older mothers is the increasing incidence of divorce and remarriage. Many women who have completed their first family split up, then remarry or live with a new partner. They want to have a child to seal the relationship. This can be especially important when the new partner has not had children before.

"When I married Clay I had two teenage children and he had a daughter, age four, from his previous marriage. We both very much wanted to have another baby although I was nearly 40. It seemed to us that having another baby would bring the whole family together. It also seemed like a good idea to provide a brother or sister for Laura, who wanted one very much."

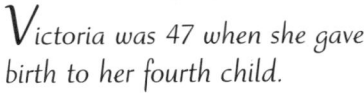

Victoria was 47 when she gave birth to her fourth child.

Victoria was 47 when she gave birth to her fourth child; her other three children from her first marriage were in their early twenties. "Sam was 14 years younger than I. We'd discussed children and decided it was fine not to have them. But I didn't like to think it would be my age that kept Sam from being a father. He was good with children—everyone's wonderful uncle and godfather. Lucky for us, it was the right thing to do. It's been wonderful for him to have a child."

⌐ Earth mothers

Another group of older mothers are those who have large families, sometimes increasing over many years. These are the "earth mothers" who find having a small baby at the breast the most fulfilling time of their lives and are reluctant to move on. Sally married at 32 and had four children, when she was 33, 35, 37 and 39. Then, unable to leave the experience behind her, she had another "last-minute" fifth child at the age of 43.

"I'm prepared to admit there might be something wrong with me, that I had all these children for my own pleasure and that I'm postponing facing up to life beyond small children, but they're all healthy, they're all happy. I believe you get to be a much better mother with experience, so I don't think anyone can really criticize me. And if anyone mentions the population problem, I just say my sister doesn't want children so she's let me have her 2.3 for her."

⌒ Afterthoughts

Other late babies are born to women after the mother has decided that her family is complete. Most of these late babies are "mistakes," or "afterthoughts," but some are planned. James and Diane had been married for 15 years and had two teenage children when Diane found out James was having an affair. "This development really shook things up. Things were fairly desperate for weeks," Diane recalls. But the couple had a strong enough relationship to withstand the hidden dissatisfactions the affair brought up. Once those had been discussed and resolved, they became closer again. "We took a second honeymoon. I suggested another baby, and to my amazement James agreed with me. Marianne was the result. She has been wonderful; she's brought nothing but joy to the whole family. She's brought all of us closer together, including the children."

⌒ Single women

A woman living on her own reaching her late 30s may decide she cannot wait any longer to find the "right man." Or she may not even want to live with a man but still want a child. More women than ever are deciding to become a parent alone, partly because social attitudes toward single mothers have become more accepting. Women may either choose to conceive through a male friend, with his consent or by stealth, or may seek artificial insemination by donor.

*M*ore women than ever are deciding to become a parent alone.

For all older women who decide to get pregnant, however, there are two main worries: Will I conceive, how long will it take—and will I be able to have a normal pregnancy and birth, and a healthy child?

2

If You Can't Get Pregnant

Infertility and late motherhood are linked in two ways. First, many women come late to motherhood because they have had trouble conceiving. Second, fertility declines with age, and many women who leave childbearing to their mid- or late 30s or early 40s experience some difficulty in getting pregnant.

Although every doctor and medical textbook will state that fertility declines with age, finding out exactly when and how fast fertility declines is not so easy. Figures from the Office of Population Censuses and Surveys show that in 1996, 400,810 women aged 35 to 39, and 74,643 women aged 40 to 49 gave birth, out of a total of 3,917,933 births for women of all ages—clearly a minority. This figure doesn't really prove anything, however. The smallness of the figure may be due more to women choosing to have their babies earlier rather than experiencing difficulty in having them later. According to the Report of Final Nativity Statistics, 1995 (National Center for Health Statistics), "Birth rates for women in their thirties is still increasing, but the pace has slowed. The birth rate for women aged 40 to 44 years rose 20% between 1990 and 1995, and increased 74% during 1981-95. The rising birth rate, along with the increasing number of women in this age group, has meant that there were more babies born in 1995 to mothers in their forties than in any year since 1966."

A study by Professor James Trussel of Princeton University, published in 1985, shows that between the years 1550 and 1849, when people did not have access to birth control, only about 7% of women who married young were infertile, while one-third of women who married at the age of 35 did not give birth and nearly

60% of women who married at 40 had no children.

When and how fast does fertility decline? One recent study to try to answer this question was carried out in the Netherlands on a group of 751 women attending clinics for artificial insemination by donated sperm. This study showed the decline in fertility began at the age of 31, and that after this age the chance of conceiving per monthly cycle fell by about 12% with each year of age. The chance of a woman aged 35 getting pregnant and giving birth to a healthy baby was about half that of a woman aged 25. The study also showed that for older women, continuing beyond 12 cycles was important, since older women took longer to conceive. While 54% of women over 31 became pregnant after 12 cycles, 75% did after 24. These figures may be slightly different compared to those found from women who conceive normally, because we know there is a slightly lower rate of conception through donor insemination than natural conception. Still, they are likely not to be much different.

Older women tend to be infertile for the same reasons as younger women, but the problems arise more frequently. The most common reason is probably a failure to ovulate. As women age, they are likely to have more menstrual cycles without ovulating than younger women; eventually most cycles will be anovulatory (menstruation without releasing an egg). Women usually continue to have periods long after they cease to be fertile, for perhaps ten years before they reach menopause.

Older women tend to be infertile for the same reasons as younger women, but the problems arise more frequently.

Older women are also more likely to have suffered from some infection or illness that might scar the Fallopian tubes, the second most common cause of female infertility. Older women are also more likely to develop fibroids or other uterine disorders that affect fertility.

Research into infertility and a host of new treatments have meant more women with fertility problems are able to have a baby than ever before. Advances such as IVF (in-vitro fertilization, the "test-tube baby" treatment) have put infertility very much in the public eye. Infertility is no longer the hush-hush issue it used to be. Because of this, many women are now aware their fertility may be a problem. They are much more likely to seek help quickly if they do not become pregnant soon after stopping contraception.

Women who have spent years on the Pill or worrying about contraception, who may never have had an act of unprotected intercourse or fretted till their period turned up if they did, may be surprised to find pregnancy does not automatically result as soon as they abandon contraception. In fact, it has been estimated that the average length of time for a fertile couple having regular sexual intercourse to conceive a baby is about six months. This means that for every lucky couple who gets pregnant the first month, another couple

The study also showed that for older women, continuing beyond 12 cycles was important, since older women took longer to conceive.

will wait a year. It's a little like throwing the dice and getting the certain number you're hoping for—your chances are the same for each throw, but over a number of throws, your number is more likely to come up.

Similarly, the chance of conceiving each month is probably the same, but for the woman in her late 30s, not conceiving right away will probably ring alarm bells. She will be aware all the time that a delay of a year in conceiving may considerably reduce her chances. She may rush off for fertility investigations before she has given her body a chance to conceive naturally.

If a couple has not conceived after a year, and especially if the mother is older, most doctors will go ahead and refer them to a fertility specialist. The specialist will decide if there is really a problem and what this might be.

⌒ How conception occurs

Human conception is a miraculous and complex event. It is perhaps more surprising that pregnancy occurs so often than that it fails sometimes. A human egg is released every month from a woman's ovary under the influence of a complex cycle of hormones. The hormones are released by the pituitary gland and the hypothalamus, located in the brain. The egg is swept into the Fallopian tubes by delicate projections (called the *fimbria*) at the end of the tubes, where it is normally fertilized by the man's sperm. The fertilized egg then moves down the tube and, helped along by the tiny hair-like cilia that line the tube, enters the uterus, or womb. The embryo must implant into the lining of the uterus (the endometrium). There it starts to produce hormones that will stimulate its growth. The site in the ovary, called the *corpus luteum,* from which the egg was released, must produce enough of the hormone progesterone to sustain the pregnancy for the first three months. After that the placenta takes over that job.

The most common cause of female infertility is failure to ovulate, and this condition is the easiest to treat.

The woman's uterus must be structurally sound and capable of expanding to contain the growing fetus. The cervix, the opening of the uterus, must be strong enough to hold in the baby until it is ready to be born.

It is estimated that it takes a fertile couple having regular sexual intercourse an average of six months to conceive. At any point, something can go wrong and pregnancy will not result:

◆ Sometimes an egg is not released.

◆ The egg and sperm may fail to meet and fertilize.

◆ Many early embryos fail to implant, and sometimes an implanted embryo fails to develop or is rejected by the mother's body.

◆ An abnormality in the fetus or a lack of sufficient levels of the hormone progesterone may make it impossible for the embryo to survive, resulting in a miscarriage.

Roughly one-third of infertility is caused by a problem in the woman, one-third by a problem in the man. Of the last one-third of cases, infertility is caused by a combination of problems in both partners or, in about 20% of these cases, is unexplained (American Society for Reproductive Medicine, "Frequently Asked Questions about Infertility," 1996). The statistics for unexplained infertility have tended to fall with better diagnosis and an improved understanding of what causes infertility, but it is still more common than many doctors like to admit.

The most common cause of female infertility is failure to ovulate, and this condition is the easiest to treat. A course of fertility drugs can be given to see if these will activate the ovaries. There are several fertility drugs, and while the doctor may know which is the best to try, often he simply has to go through each in turn, trying different doses, to see what is or is not successful. This can make the woman feel like a human guinea pig. Tests into other areas of infertility can be long, complicated and invasive. Male infertility is the hardest to treat.

⌒ Visiting a fertility clinic

If you eventually visit a fertility clinic, you and your partner will be asked for details of your medical history: any past illnesses and any surgery. You will be asked questions about your sex life: how many sexual partners you have had, how often you make love, and so on. Many people find this an intrusion into their privacy, but the questions are all relevant.

A routine physical examination will be carried out on both partners. You will be examined to check that your respective reproductive organs are normal. For the man, this means inspecting the external genitalia and in particular the testicles for any signs of a varicocele (enlarged veins) or other abnormality. The woman will have an internal pelvic examination, during which the doctor will insert a speculum to hold the walls of the vagina apart so that she can view the cervix and take swabs for testing if she suspects a vaginal infection. She will also use her hands to feel the internal organs; this may enable her to detect problems such as fibroids, ovarian cysts or scarring from previous infections.

⌒ Tests undergone by the woman

One of the first tests for infertility is to find out whether the woman is ovulating, by using basal-body-temperature charts. At the time of ovulation there is a small but distinct rise in the body's temperature, due to production of the hormone progesterone. This temperature spike can be measured by taking a woman's temperature every morning on waking up. Many women find this to be a bothersome procedure. A three-month record should show if you are ovulating and if your cycle is normal, but you may be asked to continue keeping a temperature chart much longer than this. Because temperature charts are sometimes difficult to interpret and are not always reliable, the woman will probably be given further tests to measure the level of hormones that control ovulation. Doctors may order a blood-progesterone test, a simple and painless way of measuring the level of progesterone when it reaches its peak at about day 24 in a 28-day cycle. If the level of progesterone is high, it is a good indication that ovulation has occurred.

A single sperm count is very unreliable as an indicator of a man's normal fertility.

The postcoital test may also pinpoint why a woman is not conceiving. The woman makes an appointment for the time of the month when she thinks she will be ovulating. The couple is asked to have sexual intercourse on the night before or the morning of the appointment. At the clinic, the doctor will take a sample of the woman's cervical mucus from the neck of the womb for examination. The quality of the mucus—clear and slippery, or sticky and opaque—tends to indicate whether the woman has ovulated. By examining the mucus under a microscope, it is also possible to tell if the sperm are normal, if there are enough of them and whether the sperm are agglutinated (clumping together), which might indicate the presence of antibodies. If postcoital tests are repeatedly not very good, the next step may be to test the semen and mucus for antibodies to sperm that may interfere with sperm motility (ability to move).

An endometrial biopsy is a procedure that shows whether or not the woman has ovulated. It involves taking a small sample of the lining of the womb for examination. This is a minor surgical procedure, similar to a D&C (dilitation and curettage). The test should show if the womb lining is sufficiently primed by hormones to be able to receive the egg for implantation. If the woman is ovulating normally, the next investigation will be to see if the Fallopian tubes are clear.

Doctors will take an X-ray of the uterus and Fallopian tubes. A dye is injected through the cervix and into the uterus. The dye passes through the womb, along the Fallopian tubes and into the pelvic cavity. This enables the doctor to see all the organs.

A laparoscopy is used to detect blocked or damaged tubes and other abnormalities of the womb or ovaries. Under general anesthetic, a small incision is made in the navel, and a laparoscope—a telescope-like instrument—is inserted. This instrument helps the surgeon to examine the organs in detail and assess the extent of any damage.

Sometimes a hysteroscopy is performed—an inspection of the inside of the womb with an instrument similar to a laparoscope. Ultrasound may also be used vaginally to assess the ovaries and womb.

⌒ Tests undergone by the man

The man will be asked to produce one or more sperm samples. This should be done at the outset, before the woman undergoes any major procedures. The man is asked to produce a sample by masturbation into a sterile container either in the clinic or at home. If he does this at home, he must deliver the sample to the clinic within 1-1/2 hours. The sample is examined to see if the sperm are healthy, numerous and motile. Since one test is not always reliable, a poor result may mean he has to repeat the test.

Sometimes a man is diagnosed as subfertile on the basis of one test alone. Yet a single sperm count is very unreliable as an indicator of a man's normal fertility. Sperm counts vary enormously from one act of intercourse to another. If all is well, this may be the only test the man has to undergo. If he has a very low or absent sperm count, however, he may undergo other tests to look for a cause. The sperm may also be examined at the postcoital test (see page 20), which may give some insight into why the sperm are not functioning properly.

Hormone tests may be carried out to check levels of testosterone, a male hormone. His doctor may perform a testicular biopsy. In some cases where the man has no sperm at all, or *azoospermia,* an operation may be carried out under general anesthetic to check that the *vas deferens* (the tube that transports sperm out of the testis) is not obstructed and to see whether there are any structural abnormalities.

ᷓ Aftermath of contraception

Contraceptive methods are only very rarely a cause of infertility. The interuterine device (IUD) can increase a woman's chance of suffering from pelvic inflammatory disease (PID), which can lead to infertility. The contraceptive pill sometimes leads to a condition called *post-Pill amenorrhoea,* in which a woman's periods do not return when she stops taking the Pill. Research has shown that this condition lasts for a maximum of two years after Pill use. It can also be treated with drugs.

A woman used to taking the Pill for several years, or using an IUD or cap regularly and worrying every time her period is late, may well expect to get pregnant as soon as she stops using her chosen contraception. But often she does not. This does not necessarily mean she is infertile. However, as a woman gets older her fertility declines. Using contraception for years may mean she is less fertile by the time she stops and tries to get pregnant. Also, using contraception, and particularly the Pill, can disguise infertility problems for years. The Pill usually means that a woman has a regular cycle; she may not realize she is not ovulating.

ᷓ Hormonal problems

One of the most common causes of infertility in women is a malfunctioning of the complex hormonal interactions that govern a woman's menstrual cycle. The woman's monthly cycle is controlled by the pituitary gland in the brain which, in turn, is governed by another gland called the *hypothalamus.* The pituitary produces a follicle-stimulating hormone (FSH), which controls the production of the hormone estrogen by the ovary. It also prepares one of the follicles inside the ovary to release the egg. A second pituitary hormone, luteinizing hormone (LH), enables the ovary to release its egg. Estrogen causes the lining of the womb to thicken in readiness to receive the fertilized egg.

If the egg is not fertilized, the corpus luteum begins to shrink, levels of estrogen and progesterone decrease, the lining of the womb disintegrates and menstrual bleeding results. Falling levels of estrogen and progesterone stimulate the pituitary to produce more FSH, and the cycle begins again.

If the egg is fertilized, however, and implants into the womb, the corpus luteum continues to produce estrogen and progesterone until the placenta attaching the fetus to the wall of the womb is mature enough to produce the necessary hormones itself.

Failure to ovulate is normally caused by the woman's body's failure to produce enough of the pituitary hormones, or by their release at the wrong time. Since the pituitary is ultimately controlled by the hypothalamus, anything that affects the hypothalamus can also affect this gland. The hypothalamus can be affected by severe physical and emotional stress, as many women know when the stress of travel, work, illness or emotional turmoil disrupts their menstrual cycle. As women age, fewer menstrual cycles actually involve ovulation, so that in her early forties as few as one in every two or three cycles will produce an egg.

ᕋ Treatment

Help for women unable to ovulate has been available for many years in the form of fertility drugs. There are two main types: those that prod the pituitary into producing FSH and LH on time and those that replace FSH and LH if this approach fails.

Clomiphene citrate (Clomid®) is an artificial drug that triggers the release of FSH and LH in the pituitary. It seems to induce ovulation in about 80% of women treated with it, though not all will succeed in getting pregnant. One reason for this is that clomiphene tends to prevent the cervical mucus from becoming fluid at the fertile time in the month to enable the sperm to enter the womb. This problem can sometimes be overcome by giving estrogen as well in the few days before ovulation.

Sometimes a combination of clomiphene and human chorionic gonadotrophin (HCG, a hormone produced by the placenta and young embryo) given on the fourteenth day of the cycle will induce women to ovulate who would not do so on clomiphene alone. Clomiphene also seems to help women with a progesterone deficiency. It has been in use for many years and is considered safe, although a few women do have unpleasant side effects, such as nausea, a bloated feeling, or very rarely, enlargement of the ovaries accompanied by pain in the pelvis. Some infertility specialists deny the severity of these symptoms, or fail to inform women of them. Severe symptoms may indicate over-stimulation of the ovaries.

Recently there has been some concern that clomiphene citrate might cause more eggs, which have chromosomal abnormalities, to be released following its use. Others have questioned whether there might be other long-term effects on the children who are conceived after their mothers took fertility drugs, as happened with the children of women who took the drug DES (diethylstilbestrol) in early pregnancy to prevent a miscarriage. This is of particular concern to women who take large doses of fertility drugs to make them produce more than one egg, as is done for IVF and other treatments. However, there is no evidence to support such fears yet.

Human menopausal gonadotrophin (HMG), trade name Pergonal® and Humegon™, is a hormone extracted from the urine of pregnant women. It stimulates the follicles containing the egg. HMG is usually given as a daily injection, followed by the injection of another drug, HCG, which actually triggers ovulation. About 90% of women will ovulate with this treatment, though again, not all will conceive and some will miscarry. About 20% to 30% of pregnancies resulting from this treatment will be multiple births. HMG is responsible for most of the multiple pregnancies that occur with fertility drugs.

The hormone HMG is potent and may over-stimulate the ovaries, so the level of estrogen in the blood must be monitored daily and the follicles are often monitored by ultrasound. A new development, which might overcome this problem, is a small "pump" about the size of a wallet that, attached to the woman's arm, provides small, even doses of hormone through a fine needle. However, having a pump attached day and night and having to have the needle repositioned when necessary can be unpleasant.

Some women do not ovulate because their blood contains a high level of a hormone called *prolactin,* which is normally produced in quantity only while breastfeeding and which tends to prevent ovulation. For women with this problem there may be hope with a drug called *bromocriptine.* Bromocriptine prevents the pituitary from producing prolactin, and after treatment ovulation occurs in about 95% of women who previously produced too much.

✎ Scarring or structural abnormalities

The other major causes of infertility in women are scarring of the reproductive organs by past disease or surgery, or structural abnormalities present from birth.

◆ Untreated sexually transmitted diseases, especially gonorrhea, can result in infertility. As many as 80% of infected women never have any severe symptoms with the disease, and may not realize that they have it and that infection has spread to the Fallopian tubes, causing damage.

◆ PID (pelvic inflammatory disease), which can start after an induced abortion or miscarriage, after childbirth, after surgery in the pelvic region or after infection with a sexually transmitted disease, can cause tubal scarring and blockage.

◆ Other infections that can affect fertility are chlamydia and mycoplasmas. Chlamydia, a bacterium that closely resembles a virus, has deceptively mild symptoms. An untreated "silent" infection can destroy the inside of a woman's Fallopian tubes. Mycoplasmas, another organism, may affect fertility and has been held responsible for miscarriages.

ᑎ Other causes

Endometriosis is a disease that may affect as many as 5% to 10% of women at some stage of their reproductive lives. Normally endometrial tissue lines the womb, or *endometrium*. The condition is caused by patches of the endometrial tissue becoming deposited outside the womb. This tissue, like the womb lining, thickens and bleeds with each menstrual cycle. Scar tissue is formed that may block the ends of the Fallopian tubes, or adhesions may form that prevent the tube from picking up the egg on its release from the ovary.

Endometriosis can be treated by a number of drugs: birth-control pills, progesterone or a drug called Danazol®, which blocks production of the two pituitary hormones, and now new drugs called *LHRH analogs,* which are given as a nasal spray or an injection. These treatments serve to "switch off" the menstrual cycle, stopping the patches of endometrial tissue from bleeding; then they fade away and any adhesions or scar tissue can be removed by careful surgery.

About one-third of all women have fibroids or polyps by the age of 40. These are benign swellings in the womb, usually only the size of a grape but sometimes swelling to the size of a grapefruit. Fibroids seldom cause symptoms in women who are not pregnant and rarely cause problems in pregnancy, but women with fibroids may find their fertility is affected. They can be removed by surgery. Malformations of the womb, such as the presence of a dividing wall or septum, can sometimes be corrected by surgery.

Previous surgery in the abdominal region can also be a cause of damage to the tubes. Bleeding or injury to the tissues may cause scar tissue or adhesions to form, which may block or freeze the tubes, ovaries or uterus in unnatural positions. That makes it impossible for the egg to pass from the ovaries into the Fallopian tubes, so conception becomes impossible.

More women with blocked Fallopian tubes have a better chance to achieve pregnancy today because doctors are practicing delicate microsurgeries with increasing skill. However, if surgery is not effective, there is still hope through the test-tube baby treatment or IVF (see chapter 4).

Occasionally a fertilized egg fails to move through the tube and into the uterus. Instead, it grows in the tube. Eventually the pregnancy will abort, or the egg may burst the tube, causing considerable bleeding and damage. This is called an *ectopic* or *tubal pregnancy.* It results in both the loss of one pregnancy and a possible barrier to future conception. One Fallopian tube is often lost. The other may be damaged by bleeding caused by the ruptured tube, or by the surgery to remove the pregnancy. It is estimated that about half the women who have an ectopic pregnancy may never conceive again. Increasingly, delicate surgery by laparoscopy may be able to save a tube, however.

Often an ectopic pregnancy occurs when there has been some damage to the tube, perhaps caused by past infections or surgery. Tubal pregnancy is also more common if a woman becomes pregnant with an IUD in place or has been using the progestogen-only (or "mini") Pill. An ectopic pregnancy is very painful and can be life-threatening. However, prompt medical attention to remove the developing embryo before the tube can burst avoids many risks and improves the chances of successfully reconstructing the damaged tube.

⌒ Causes of male infertility

Men's fertility also falls with age, but more slowly and later than it does in women. Since most older mothers have partners the same age or older, male infertility can exert its own effect. A combination of slightly lowered fertility in both partners can combine to make pregnancy less likely.

Male infertility can be caused by blocked tubes. These tubes, called the *vasa deferentia,* carry sperm from the testes, where they are made, to the penis. Tubes can be blocked from birth because of a congenital defect, through scarring caused by sexually transmitted diseases, and through surgery, as in a vasectomy. An increasing number of men choose vasectomy once their families are complete, but if the marriage breaks up and they remarry, vasectomy can be the cause of infertility in the second marriage.

Male infertility can also be caused by:

◆ Undescended testicles. If these are not diagnosed early in a boy's life, permanent infertility will result.

◆ Infections involving the testicles. Orchitis, inflammation of the testicles following mumps, can result in infertility rarely.

◆ Varicocele. A "varicose vein" of the testicle; it may be a cause of male infertility.

◆ Disorders of ejaculation. Sometimes, as a result of illness, such as diabetes, or surgery, such as a prostatectomy, sperm is ejaculated backwards into the bladder at orgasm.

◆ Low sperm count, or a large proportion of the man's sperm being abnormal. Although research is being done, no one really understands what causes low sperm counts. However, their origin is believed to be hormonal.

ᗡ Treatments

Because so little is understood about the causes of much male infertility, only limited help is available for the majority of men with a low or absent sperm count. Some causes are known (see above) but there is little that can be done about them.

One form of male infertility can be caused by a varicocele, or varicose vein, around the testicle. This can be treated, although its link with infertility has been questioned. A simple operation to tie off the vein may improve sperm quantity and quality in about two-thirds of cases, thus increasing the chances of conception.

Blocked or scarred vasa deferentia, especially after vasectomy, may be restored surgically but there is only a 50% success rate. A man with blocked tubes often produces antibodies to the sperm because they cannot be ejaculated and have to be reabsorbed by the body. A procedure called *percutaneous epididymal sperm aspiration* can now remove sperm from the testes, and they are used to fertilize an egg.

Other causes of a low sperm count are resistant to treatment. Various hormone treatments have been tried, with a low success rate. Some studies have shown the success rate is actually lower among treated men than among those who have not received any drugs at all. Many of the drugs—some of which are the same as female fertility drugs—also have unpleasant side effects, such as loss of libido, swollen breasts or loss of body hair. To a man whose self-esteem is already dented by the fact of his infertility, these side effects can be impossible to bear, and such treatments are used rarely today.

One new technique that may help men with a low sperm count is the split-ejaculate technique. The first part of several ejaculates—the part richest in sperm—is pooled and introduced into the vagina through artificial insemination. (This may not work where a large number of abnormal sperm are present.)

Now IVF and similar techniques, such as GIFT (gamete intrafallopian transfer), offer new hope for subfertile men (see pages 30 to 36 for full details). Far fewer sperm are needed to achieve fertilization in vitro, because the sperm do not have to make their arduous journey through the vagina, cervix, uterus and tubes, with most being left behind at one point or another. Sometimes sperm are capable of fertilizing an egg but not of penetrating the cervix or surviving long in the woman's reproductive tract. By mixing sperm directly with the egg, as in IVF, these problems may be overcome. A new technique that may offer hope is called *intra-cytoplasmic sperm injection,* or ICSI, where a single sperm is injected into the egg.

⤸ Other help

Some men can improve their sperm counts by consuming a more healthful diet, by stopping or reducing smoking and drinking alcohol, by avoiding hot baths and not wearing tight underwear. Since the testes are sensitive to heat, men who work in a very hot environment may experience a reduced fertility.

Sperm counts can also be lowered by illness, especially those involving a fever. In those cases, sperm counts may be reduced for some time afterwards because it takes three months for sperm to be produced in the body. Fortunately, this is a short-term problem that will resolve itself.

If the sperm count is consistently so low that conception is very unlikely, the main alternative with male infertility is artificial insemination by donor or donor insemination (DI). This is not a cure for infertility, but it does enable a woman with an infertile partner to conceive and bear a child. In DI, semen is donated by an anonymous donor. The semen has been screened to verify it does not contain any infectious diseases. Then it is introduced through a tube into the woman's vagina, close to the cervix, by a doctor or nurse. Donors are screened carefully. There is usually an attempt to match the donor's physical characteristics with that of the woman's partner.

It can be difficult to decide when to stop treatments.

The woman goes to the clinic once a month at the most fertile time in her cycle (this is usually worked out with temperature charts). If her periods are irregular, she may be given ovulation-inducing drugs so the doctors will be able to predict the best time for insemination. The woman is usually advised to lie on her back for about half an hour to enable the sperm to swim into the uterus. Rates of conception with DI seem to be about the same as with ordinary sexual intercourse.

Going through the tests and treatments already described is in itself a remarkable testament to most couple's desire for a child. By the time these couples consider the new assisted-reproduction techniques, they have probably been through months or years of tests and the more orthodox fertility treatments. At the same time, it can be difficult to decide when to stop. "You feel you've already invested so many years and so much pain in all this, you just have to follow through to the end," said one woman undergoing fertility treatment.

In-vitro fertilization (IVF)

Of all the new fertility treatments that have been developed, IVF has had the greatest impact. Since the dramatic news of the birth of baby Louise Brown in England on July 25, 1978, IVF has given new hope to women who previously had no hope of a baby due to blocked or scarred Fallopian tubes. At the same time, it is important to remember that IVF is demanding in terms of time and emotional stress. It is expensive, is not readily available, and the failure rate is still high.

The success rate of IVF varies, but the most accurate figures show that just over 10% of all treatments actually result in a live baby. In specialist centers where larger numbers of IVF treatments are performed, the success rate is higher than in small centers, and the success rates also depend on the age of the women treated. If the treatment is at least a partial success—for example, the embryo may be fertilized and divide normally but fail to implant, or the woman might have an early miscarriage—most centers will probably give the woman another chance, but few recommend more than three or four attempts. The success rate of IVF also decreases with the woman's age, especially once a woman reaches the age of 39. Official figures show that live birth rates per cycle went from 16% of women aged 25 to 34, to 11% of women aged 35 to 39, to 5% of women aged 40 to 44. When donated eggs were used, the figures were higher.

IVF is a lengthy process. First, the woman's menstrual cycle has to be controlled with drugs such as clomiphene or HMG (Pergonal or Humegon) to ensure she will ovulate at the right time for treatment. Drugs are usually used to stimulate her ovaries to produce more than one egg at a time. To do this, the woman's hormone levels have to be carefully monitored by blood tests and often by ultrasound scanning. This is done so that several eggs can be fertilized at once, increasing the chance of success. Also, more than one embryo may be transferred, to increase the chance of at least one implanting and developing further.

The woman then goes into the hospital for an egg-retrieval operation, which involves a local and sedation anesthesia. A gas is pumped into her abdomen and an instrument called a *laparoscope* is introduced through a small incision in her abdomen. With the laparoscope, the doctor views the ovaries and can remove any ripe eggs from the follicles. Today, vaginal egg collection is sometimes done. The retrieved eggs are kept in a special culture fluid to allow them to mature. Then they are fertilized with the husband's sperm, which he is expected to produce by masturbation. Fresh semen is used if possible, because this increases the chance of success slightly, but under the stress of the procedure some men are unable to produce any. For this reason, sometimes semen is collected earlier and frozen in readiness for use at the appropriate time.

The sperm and eggs are mixed in the special culture solution to aid fertilization. If fertilization does take place, the embryos are allowed to develop for two or three days, so doctors can make sure development is normal. The embryos then are introduced into the woman's uterus in a process usually called *embryo transfer*. When the eggs are ready to be transferred, the woman will have to lie on her back with legs raised while the doctor passes a sterile catheter containing the culture fluid and embryos through the cervix (neck of the uterus). This procedure is usually done with the help of ultrasound monitoring. A mild sedative may be given to help the woman relax during this procedure, because passing anything through the cervix can be uncom-fortable. Following the transfer, most women are asked to rest in bed for 10 to 30 minutes before leaving the clinic.

If there is a choice of embryos available, only the best will be introduced. If not, some embryos that appear less suitable may be used, because they do sometimes develop normally and produce a healthy baby. Most abnormal embryos are lost early. There is no evidence that babies born through IVF are any more likely to have serious health problems than those conceived naturally.

Over a period of months or years, attempts to conceive with the help of IVF can take over a couple's life. For the woman, it can be difficult to keep a job or do anything else while IVF is being attempted. The frequent disappointments can seem over-whelming. Many mothers also find the existence of IVF, and the opportunity it represents, makes it harder to "let go" and accept childlessness, or, if they already have one child, that their child will never have a brother or sister.

In GIFT, eggs and sperm are collected in the same way as in IVF. But then the eggs and sperm are reintroduced together into the Fallopian tube, through the uterus, in a process similar to embryo transfer. It is hoped fertilization will take place naturally. This procedure does not require sophisticated equipment for embryo culture. The embryo is formed not in a culture medium but in the woman's own tubal fluid. This may mean there is a greater chance of the embryo developing normally and implanting.

GIFT can only be used when the woman still has one functioning Fallopian tube, so it is not an alternative to IVF. It is normally used when no reason can be found for infertility (unexplained infertility) or when there is evidence the woman's cervix is hostile to the man's sperm, or the sperm are failing to make it to the egg. Success rates of 25% to 30% have been claimed, but in reality the success rate is likely to be similar to that of

GIFT *(gamete intrafallopian transfer) uses a lot of the same technology as IVF but it is a newer, simpler procedure.*

IVF. In cases of male infertility, IVF is probably preferable to GIFT.

Some experts feel GIFT is used too often for couples with unexplained infertility, who have no signs of abnormalities and might conceive normally. One example is Jenny, who had her first son at 33. Two years later, she and her husband decided to try for another baby but seven months later, when nothing had happened, they went for fertility tests. Her husband Tom was told his sperm count was on the low side, but after he had given up alcohol, tried acupuncture and generally improved his level of fitness, they were told there wasn't a problem. "All the time there was hope; after all, we had had Jake. Time was marching on; Jake was four, I was nearly 38, and still no baby. I felt some pressure. We tried GIFT, but this was very invasive, stressful and didn't work. My whole life was consumed with treatment and worrying about having a second baby. I worried that Jake was missing out. Once I reached 40 I decided just to give up. Soon after, I discovered I was pregnant with Bradley, who was born safely when I was 41. Who knows whether I could have become pregnant sooner if we hadn't been messing around with GIFT?"

Because most infertility treatments do become less successful with age, some doctors and clinics may decline to treat women over 40. However, some doctors strongly disagree with this policy and will treat women regardless of age if they believe the woman has a strong argument in her favor, and there is no reason why she shouldn't have a baby.

If a woman cannot use her own eggs because the chance of

pregnancy is too low, she may succeed with donor eggs. This leads to a situation in which a woman may give birth to a child who is genetically not her own. When donor eggs are used, the embryos are likely to be of better quality and more likely to implant. The risks of a multiple pregnancy in an older-age woman are very real with this method.

The new treatment of using egg donation in women who have had premature menopause or indeed in menopausal women up to the age of 50 was first used in Britain in 1986. The first mother gave birth to twins at 46; the second was 43. Research has shown that, provided a woman has no problems with her uterus and she responds well to hormone-replacement therapy, the success rate following egg donation can be high. The oldest woman to date to give birth, in Los Angeles in 1997, was 63. She relied on a donated egg and her husband's sperm.

The success rate when donor eggs are used seems to depend more on the age of the donor than on the woman who receives the egg. In particular, miscarriage rates are the same as those of younger women rather than the higher rates usually found in older mothers.

Following the success of egg donation in helping women in their 40s to conceive, other doctors—notably Professor Severino Antinori in Rome and Dr. Mark Sauer at the University of Southern California—have used the same treatment on women in their fifties with great success.

The success rate when donor eggs are used seems to depend more on the age of the donor than on the woman who receives the egg.

Many criticize the treatment because it overturns the "natural" order—although we know that it can be natural for a woman to conceive as late as 57. But how many women will want to choose that option? Women who have suffered infertility problems for years and given up the hope of ever having a baby may now be able to step forward and receive help. This was the case with Giuseppina Maganuco, a 54-year-old homemaker from Sicily, who had spent years unsuccessfully trying to conceive. She had had surgery for blocked Fallopian tubes before being told she was too old to have a baby. Dr. Antinori used donated eggs mixed with her husband's sperm to achieve the birth of baby Anna Maria in December 1991.

Using donor eggs raises further ethical considerations. They have been used for various infertility treatments, where the woman has no ovaries but has a healthy uterus, where her eggs are unsuitable for transfer in IVF, or where she has some genetic abnormality she does not want passed on to her children. Donating eggs involves the donor going through the IVF procedure except for the embryo transfer. She takes fertility drugs to induce her to produce more than one egg for donation, and she has to undergo a minor operation—called a *laparotomy*—to collect the eggs. She must be highly motivated to agree to these procedures. Some women who have experienced fertility problems themselves donate eggs, as do sisters, friends or other relatives of the infertile woman. Some doctors are wary of using eggs from close relatives because they fear this may cause stress in the family and confusion in the child as to his or her "real" mother; however, unknown donors are hard to find.

Christine became an egg donor in 1991 when her friend Jane was turned down for egg donation at a private fertility clinic. "They told her that, at 41, she was too old and that they would only give the treatment to a younger woman for whom the chances of success were higher. This was the end of a long saga of fertility problems and miscarriages; she had also been turned down by adoption agencies because of her age.

"I asked her if they would do an egg donation if she found a donor and offered myself. They were reluctant; we had to bully them into it. I had to have counseling to make sure I understood what I was doing, and I had to sign a piece of paper waiving all my rights to the eggs. I had an AIDS test, and I had to have a course of ten injections and use a nasal spray every four hours or so. My cycle had to be synchronized with hers so they could use some of the eggs fresh to increase her chances.

"I did the injections myself, every morning in my rear, for ten days. I had to remember to use the nasal spray, which I didn't like. I had some pain in my ovaries due to the large number of eggs that were developing. Then I went in, had another large injection and a scan—I could see they had nine eggs on one side and three on the other—and a light general anesthetic while they brought out the eggs.

"At the time I did think about it a lot. I told myself, it's not a child, its just an egg, but if Jane had gotten pregnant . . . I think I would have wanted to see the child and know how he or she was doing, especially since I knew Jane. When she failed to get pregnant I was very disappointed, for her and for me, because I had been through something big myself. She wanted me to try again but I didn't want to. It's too much and it isn't pleasant. I told her at the beginning I'd do it once and that was all. It also stirred up a lot of emotions in my family. My mother said she was relieved not to have a grandchild out there she'd never see. And to be honest, I'm a little relieved myself now."

Surrogate motherhood

One option for the older mother who is unable to conceive a child herself, or who perhaps has abnormalities of the womb that mean she cannot carry a child, is surrogate motherhood. Enormous publicity was given to the first surrogate mothers (also called *gestational carriers*), including the infamous "Baby M" case in New Jersey, where one couple commissioned Mary Beth Whitehead to have a baby for them. She changed her mind and took the baby back. Since that time, a small number of surrogate mothers have continued to have babies for infertile women. Sometimes the surrogate mother is a friend or relative of the infertile woman, although occasionally money does change hands (but commercial surrogacy is illegal).

Surrogate mothers have been used either for full surrogacy . . . or partial surrogacy.

Surrogate mothers have been used either for full surrogacy—where the infertile woman's egg is fertilized by her partner's sperm and introduced into the surrogate mother's womb—or partial surrogacy, where the surrogate mother's egg is used. Surrogacy is perhaps more common when the infertile woman is older and her chances of achieving a pregnancy in any other way are slim.

It is advisable for all parties, when undertaking this procedure, to consult with and retain legal counsel. This is to ensure that, when the child is born, it can and will be registered to the intended parents.

⌒ Adoption

Adoption is the main alternative path to motherhood for those who cannot have their own baby.

Older mothers, however, may face more difficulties adopting a baby. In the United States and Canada, adoption requirements vary from state to state and province to province, and from agency to agency as well. Many agencies set the limit of a 40-year span between the age of one of the adoptive parents and the child's age. A couple in which one partner is 50 years old and one is 42 years old would not automatically be prohibited from adopting a 3-year-old child on the basis of age, for example.

Some parents, unable to adopt at home, have adopted from overseas, where there may be large numbers of babies and young children in orphanages. The laws of the countries from which they adopt, and the rules of foreign adoption agencies, may be less restrictive. Here too, however, regulations vary from country to country and agency to agency.

Despite the relative lack of babies available for adoption, many thousands of older children in foster care are available for adoption and are seeking families. While many of them show behavioral problems and have had unhappy and disrupted childhoods, many parents who do adopt them find great fulfillment in the challenge of meeting these children's needs and participating in the joys and heartaches of parenthood.

3

Pregnant at Last

Women who have spent some time considering pregnancy in general want to make sure they are in the best health and have done everything possible to ensure they have a healthy child. Older women in particular may be anxious to do everything they can to offset the possible risks involved in being an older mother. You *can* take practical steps in advance to prepare yourself for the healthiest possible pregnancy.

It's important to check that you are immune to rubella (German measles) before you start trying to conceive. Catching this disease, particularly in the first months of pregnancy, causes severe disabilities in the child or a miscarriage. If you are not immune, you can be vaccinated against rubella before you conceive. It is also a good idea to check whether you may be carrying a sexually transmitted disease. Hard-to-diagnose infections such as chlamydia, gardnerella and mycoplasmas may be implicated in miscarriage and premature delivery. Blood tests for viruses such as cytomegalovirus, which can cause abnormalities in the baby, may also be worthwhile.

∽ Stopping contraception

If you have been relying on an IUD, you will need to have it removed by a doctor before you conceive. As soon as an IUD is removed, you can get pregnant. If you get pregnant by chance with an IUD in place, it does carry risks for mother and baby. You are more likely to have an ectopic pregnancy—a pregnancy that occurs outside the womb, usually in the Fallopian tubes—and there is a high risk of miscarriage. As many as 60% of such pregnancies end before term. The miscarriages are more likely to occur in the second three months of pregnancy. IUDs are usually removed while you have a period, because the cervix is slightly dilated then and this aids removal.

If you have been taking the Pill, stop taking it two or three months before you wish to conceive. You can use a barrier method, such as the condom or diaphragm, or natural family planning (rhythm method) during this time. (But be aware you are *unlikely to use natural family planning effectively* if you have not spent some time learning the technique and observing your menstrual cycle.) Studies have shown that women who took the Pill inadvertently in early pregnancy have only a very slight extra risk of having an abnormal pregnancy or a child with disabilities. Those who conceive as soon as they stop taking the Pill face no extra risk.

All the same, it is a good precaution to make sure that your body is free of all drugs before you get pregnant. It also helps to date the pregnancy if you have had one or two normal menstrual cycles before you conceive because this allows for good pregnancy care.

There is, however, some evidence that women who conceive while using spermicides, whether on their own or in combination with the diaphragm, cap or condom, run a slightly higher risk of a miscarriage (and, incidentally, also a greater chance of having a girl). It is obviously better to conceive when there are no traces of spermicide in the vagina. If you intend to try to conceive, it may be a good idea to ask your doctor to do a cervical smear and perhaps to take a swab to check that you do not have any vaginal infection, such as thrush, before you get pregnant. This will usually be done at your first prenatal appointment when you are pregnant anyway, but some women prefer not to have a vaginal examination in early pregnancy, especially if they have had a miscarriage or threatened miscarriage in the past. It also makes sense to clear up any infection before rather than after a pregnancy has begun.

⌐ Avoiding drugs in pregnancy

Most women are aware that taking any drugs—including tobacco and alcohol—during pregnancy can have a harmful effect on the growing and developing baby. This is especially important in the first three months, when the baby is actually forming, because this is the time when most abnormalities would occur. However, researchers have learned recently that alcohol taken at any time during pregnancy may permanently affect the child, because the brain continues to mature throughout the nine months of pregnancy. Women and their partners who are planning a pregnancy, therefore, need to give up smoking and drinking, ensure that their diet contains all the elements necessary for the baby's healthy growth, and stop any unnecessary medication. Any woman taking drugs essential for her health—for diabetes, epilepsy or high blood pressure, for example—should discuss this matter very carefully with her doctor, preferably before becoming pregnant.

Older mothers are more likely than younger ones to have an underlying health problem. If this is the case for you, then you need to find out what your best options are before you get pregnant. Some drugs will be essential for your health, but carry a small risk of affecting the baby. This was the case for Lisa:

"I have epilepsy, and I was told it was important to continue taking my drugs, because a seizure during pregnancy can be very harmful to the baby. I was told there was a very small risk of it causing an abnormality, such as cleft palate or harelip; but in my case, Thomas was born perfect and healthy."

There is evidence that heavy smoking or drinking by the father before conception can affect the quantity and quality of his sperm, and certain drugs may also affect sperm production. So some men may need to think about this too. Sperm production takes about three months, so the father should also be thinking about changing some of his habits three or four months before you plan to get pregnant.

ᥕ Alcohol

A number of studies have been done about the effect of taking alcohol during pregnancy. There is now no doubt that drinking in pregnancy can have very serious effects on the baby, at its worst causing what is known as *fetal alcohol syndrome (FAS)*. Such babies have low birth weight, and do not catch up as do the babies of malnourished mothers or babies who have not been receiving enough nourishment in the womb. Their head circumference is smaller, and there is often mental retardation and lasting behavioral problems. Some have odd facial characteristics. Drinking during pregnancy may also cause fetal alcohol effects (FAE). While causing less obvious facial and other physical characteristics, FAE is insidious because it is associated with persistent behavioral and attention-deficit disorders, which may be difficult to diagnose in older children and adults in particular.

There is a higher incidence of congenital heart disease and other abnormalities among babies born to women who drink. The greater the level of alcohol drunk by the mother, the more severe the abnormalities are likely to be and the greater the risk of the baby being miscarried or stillborn.

Doctors and health experts now advise that women not drink at all in pregnancy. The best thing to do is give up all alcohol while you are trying to conceive and for the next nine months.

There is evidence that women who do not drink at all in pregnancy are less likely to have miscarriages or low-birth-weight babies. Doctors and health experts now advise that women not drink at all in pregnancy. The best thing to do is give up all alcohol while you are trying to conceive and for the next nine months. For most older women who want a healthy baby, this won't seem too much of a hardship.

⌒ Cigarettes

Smoking in pregnancy is clearly linked to a higher risk of miscarriage and to low birth weight. Some recent evidence links congenital abnormalities with smoking. The risk of the baby being stillborn or dying in the first few weeks of life is definitely greater when the mother smokes. Babies are also much more likely to be born prematurely in this case.

If you are a smoker, the best time to stop is *before* you get pregnant. However, giving up cigarettes is not easy. Women who smoke do so for reasons that are important to them. Some women say it helps them relax; others, that it keeps their weight down. The older you are, the more at risk you are from smoking, so it's twice as important to stop. Of course, the desire for a healthy baby provides an excellent incentive for quitting.

Many women find the best way to give up smoking is to substitute with something else in its place. If you smoke to relieve stress, try yoga for relaxation or some other form of exercise. If your weight really is a problem, make sure to read all the advice about the importance of diet in pregnancy in this book (pages 46-53). Following a sensible eating plan should ensure you do not gain unnecessary pounds. If your partner smokes, try to stop together—his moral support will boost your will power and set the scene for a smoke-free household when the baby arrives. Or find a friend who also wants to stop smoking and give each other positive support.

The desire for a healthy baby provides an excellent incentive for quitting smoking.

Many people who smoke started as adolescents and have always identified themselves strongly as "smokers." It may help, as soon as you have quit, to identify yourself as a "nonsmoker" and to tell everyone you know that you have stopped smoking. Contact your local Lung Association or Heart Association for additional help. There may be a support group you can join. Your healthcare professional can be a tremendous ally also and may have some very specific strategies to suggest that can help you quit for good.

ᴄ⁊ Painkillers

Aspirin is probably the most commonly used of all drugs. Its use is so common that many people do not take it seriously as a drug at all. Aspirin is known to cross the placenta into the baby's bloodstream, but its effects on the baby are not really known. Some studies, however, have shown that aspirin in large quantities may increase the risk of miscarriage in the first three months and have other harmful effects later on, so use aspirin sparingly in pregnancy. Discuss it with your doctor before you take it while pregnant.

Acetominophen (trade name Tylenol®), is an over-the-counter drug used to relieve pain and reduce fever. It is known to affect the liver and kidneys if taken in large quantities and could affect the developing fetus. Use it only sparingly in pregnancy, and discuss it with your doctor before you take it.

Talk with your doctor about taking *any* over-the-counter or prescribed painkiller *before* you take it. Some are not safe to use during pregnancy because they could affect your unborn child.

ᕲ Tranquilizers

There has been evidence that some tranquilizers cause an increase in birth defects, notably in cleft lip and cleft palate. The evidence is not clear, but wherever possible, avoid tranquilizers during pregnancy, especially in the first three months. Discuss it with your doctor before you take anything.

ᕲ Antibiotics

Some antibiotics are known to be safe in pregnancy; others are definitely harmful. Penicillin is thought to be safe. Tetracycline causes yellow discoloration of the baby's teeth and may affect the growth of bones and teeth. Streptomycin may be linked to deafness. Always make sure any doctor prescribing antibiotics for you is aware that you are pregnant.

ᕲ Hormonal drugs

Evidence shows that women who have taken the contraceptive pill inadvertently early in pregnancy are not at any substantial risk of affecting the baby. Women who used postcoital hormonal contraception that failed also do not seem to be at risk.

Other hormonal drugs given early in pregnancy, however, do have very definite harmful effects. Hormones given in some kinds of pregnancy tests (now withdrawn from the market) caused baby girls to develop male characteristics. A drug called DES (diethylstilbestrol), given early in pregnancy to prevent miscarriage, is now known to be linked to a rare vaginal cancer in babies born to these mothers, together with some abnormalities of the internal sex organs. Other hormones, such as progestogens, given in pregnancy to prevent miscarriage or for other problems, may have harmful effects and should be avoided, although there is no conclusive evidence to prove this. In some cases where a woman has miscarried because of low hormone levels, treatment with such drugs may be justified.

✍ Anti-nausea drugs

The use of anti-nausea drugs in pregnancy is controversial. Because the baby is so vulnerable to drugs, especially in the first three months of pregnancy when nausea occurs, taking any kind of drug must be considered a last resort, for only very serious cases. Do not take any kind of medication for nausea or vomiting without the consent of your doctor.

"I had terrible nausea and vomiting in both my pregnancies. In the second pregnancy it was worse, and lasted from the fifth week (that was how I knew I was pregnant) to the sixteenth. I felt sick every minute, and I vomited frequently—two or three times some days, only once on others. It wasn't just in the morning. It was all the time and was worse when I didn't eat regular, small snacks and meals. At around seven or eight weeks I had 48 hours when I couldn't keep anything down, and because I had an active toddler to look after, I was getting desperate.

"I called my doctor, who suggested an anti-nausea drug. I was tempted, but in the end I said 'No.' The vomiting did get better after that acute phase. I did manage to eat, although I lost weight over the first three months. After 16 weeks I got dramatically better. I was very pleased to have gotten through without using drugs. If I'd taken anything, I know I would have worried for the rest of the pregnancy that something would be wrong with the baby. I wish doctors would help give you confidence to go without drugs unless you really can't keep anything down at all."

Some women do experience such severe nausea that they need extra help. Severe nausea and vomiting, called *hyperemesis gravidarum,* causes dehydration and a nutritional loss. A doctor will diagnose this condition. Women with this condition may be hospitalized and given medications and fluids intravenously.

There are alternatives to drugs, including herbal drinks or homeopathic remedies, which some women find helpful with nausea and vomiting. Ginger tea may help relieve nausea, for example. But the best way to cope with nausea and vomiting seems to be to pay careful attention to diet, which should consist of nutritious foods such as whole-grain bread, fresh fruit, nuts, raisins and dried fruit, raw vegetables and cereals. Granola bars can be good if you want something sweet.

Eating small amounts frequently helps. Fatty or very sweet foods are likely to make you feel worse rather than better. Also avoid spicy food, alcohol or cigarette smoke. If preparing food makes you feel sick, get someone else to do it for you if possible, or make meals that need minimum preparation. Drink plenty of (mainly fresh) fruit juices, herbal teas and water; avoid tea and coffee. Many people find milky drinks make sickness worse, too. Remember to keep on eating, no matter what. Believe it or not, it is much more unpleasant to be sick on an empty stomach than it is on a full one. Starving yourself is likely to make the nausea much worse. Even if food stays in the stomach only a short time, some nutrients will have been absorbed.

Ginger tea may help relieve nausea.

Alternative medicine, such as homeopathy or acupuncture, may be helpful. You could also try some specially designed elastic bands covered with soft material, which are worn around the wrists to put pressure on certain points. These are supposed to help relieve travel or morning sickness.

✎ Diet during pregnancy

Maintaining a healthy diet during pregnancy is the best thing you can do for yourself and your baby. Junk food can be harmful in pregnancy because it does not provide enough of the vitamins and nutrients the growing baby needs. It is also high in salt and other additives. That increases stress on the liver and kidneys, which have to eliminate the excess sodium from the body. If you eat the right foods, you will be doing the best for your baby. Your doctor may have you take a prenatal vitamin in addition. Be careful of taking large quantities of vitamin supplements otherwise, because some vitamins, notably vitamin A, can be harmful if taken in excess. Also, if you eat healthfully you won't need to worry about whether you're putting on the right amount of weight or not; your body will do that automatically.

⌒ Weight gain

It is normal to gain weight in pregnancy. Most additional weight appears during the second three months. The increased weight is the weight of the baby, the placenta, the waters surrounding the baby, increased fluid and tissue in the breasts as they prepare to produce milk, and a greater quantity of blood circulating in the body. Some women also experience fluid retention, which will adjust itself after the baby is born.

A normal weight gain during pregnancy is 20 to 30 pounds (9 to 13.5 kg). Some women gain less, others more—this can be normal, too. If you are planning to breast-feed your baby, remember that you will be laying down some stores of fat to feed your new baby and that the pounds will roll off as you produce milk.

Doctors used to worry a lot about "excessive" weight gain in pregnancy, because it can put an additional strain on the body, making high blood pressure and cardiovascular problems more likely. However, this situation was largely a reaction to the exhortations previously made to women to "eat for two;" that is, very heartily. But aiming for the other extreme and trying to stay slim in pregnancy is equally harmful.

It is particularly damaging to try to diet and lose weight in pregnancy unless you are overweight and under medical supervision, because you may be denying your baby vital nourishment. Again, *eating the right food is the key*. If you eat well, you will feel well, be less inclined to want to "fill up" on sweet things, and your body will gain and shed weight naturally during and after the pregnancy.

ᓭ A healthful diet

A healthful diet means eating a balanced combination of proteins, carbohydrates, fats and vitamins. This can be achieved by eating reasonable quantities of fresh meat and fish, eggs, pasteurized cheese and milk, fresh fruits and vegetables, whole-grain bread and cereals. Fresh green vegetables in particular are full of the minerals and vitamins your body and your baby need.

Avoid Junk Food

Avoid foods with "empty" calories, such as:

- ❖ Highly refined, sugary cakes and other desserts
- ❖ Sweet carbonated drinks
- ❖ Cookies
- ❖ Fried and fatty foods, such as potato chips and creamy dips
- ❖ Salty foods (they encourage fluid retention)
- ❖ Drinks such as coffee, tea and cocoa
- ❖ All alcoholic beverages

ᓭ What you need and why

ᓮ Protein

Proteins contain the basic building blocks that make up your body. These building blocks are absolutely vital during pregnancy for the baby to grow and develop. Your protein requirements increase by about 50% during pregnancy. The best sources of protein are meat and fish, dairy products, eggs, beans and some green vegetables—lentils, peas, beans, seeds, nuts and yeast are all very rich in protein. If you are a vegetarian you can still get enough protein from the latter foods, but some vegetarian women choose to eat a little fish and chicken in pregnancy to boost their protein intake. Fish is particularly valuable, because it contains a lot of minerals and vitamins and is also low in fat.

⌒ *Carbohydrates*

Carbohydrates are vital to meeting your energy needs in pregnancy. They do not have to be fattening: potatoes, especially if baked in their skins, are not fattening (they also contain a lot of vitamin C). Bread, flour, cereals and root vegetables are all good sources of carbohydrate. It's best not to skip these at mealtimes; you may feel hungry again soon after eating and fill up on junk food instead.

⌒ *Fat*

You do not need extra fat in pregnancy. If you are gaining excessive weight you can cut down on butter, oils and sauces, and indulge in low-fat yogurts and cottage cheese. However, be careful that you do not lack important fat-soluble vitamins as a result. If you are unsure, check with your doctor.

⌒ *Minerals*

A number of minerals are known to be essential for health, especially during pregnancy. Because the body's blood volume increases so much, iron is in extra demand during pregnancy. This is especially true in second and subsequent pregnancies, particularly if there has not been a long gap since the last baby was born. You can increase iron in the blood by eating iron-rich foods, notably dark-green vegetables such as spinach and watercress, liver (but some mothers may be advised to avoid liver), egg yolks, whole grains, beans and nuts, and nut spreads such as peanut butter. Your hemoglobin levels will be checked in pregnancy to make sure you are not becoming anemic. If you are, your doctor may prescribe iron pills.

Calcium is important in pregnancy for the formation of bones and teeth and to ensure blood clotting. Milk and dairy foods are a good source, but so are vegetables, whole grains, beans and nuts. Spinach, rhubarb and cocoa block calcium absorption, so do not have too much of these foods. Potassium, zinc and other trace elements are also important. Seafood is a good source of many minerals. Oysters are particularly rich in zinc.

Vitamins — Good for You

Nutrient	Rich sources	Good sources	What it does
Vitamin A	Egg yolk, oily fish, milk, butter, carrots	Liver, green and yellow vegetables	Helps resist infection, essential for vision, keeps hair and nails in good condition
Vitamin B1 Thiamine	Wheat germ, nuts, pork	Oatmeal, liver, peas, whole-wheat bread	Aids digestion, necessary for growth
Vitamin B2 Riboflavin	Brewer's yeast, wheat germ	Green vegetables, milk, eggs, liver	Builds brain cells, prevents infections and bleeding gums
Niacin	Liver, peanuts, salmon, sardines	Cooked meats, mackerel, other fish	Prevents eye and skin problems, essential for normal growth and development
Vitamin B6 Pyridoxine	Yeast, liver, mackerel	Meat, fish, eggs, banana, pineapple, whole-wheat bread	Deficiency causes disease of the nerves and anemia

Vitamin B12	Liver, sardines, herring	Turkey, tuna, salmon, beef, lamb, egg	Necessary to form red blood cells and nervous system
Folic acid	Liver, dark-green vegetables	Peanuts, walnuts, wheat germ, eggs, lettuce, mushroom, tomatoes, oranges	Same as vitamin B12. Deficiency linked to spina bifida
Vitamin C Ascorbic Acid	Strawberries, broccoli, sprouts, cabbage	Oranges, lemons, fava beans, asparagus	Helps iron absorption, important for healing
Calcium	Milk, hard cheese	Small whole fish, especially shellfish, soy, figs, peanuts, walnuts	Essential for healthy bones and teeth
Iron	Liver, beef, soy, oysters, spinach	Lamb, chicken, turkey, ham	Essential for formation of red blood cells
Zinc	Oysters, wheat germ, wheat bran	Beef, lamb, liver, cheese, milk, oatmeal, whole-grain cereals	Helps form many enzymes and proteins

Table 3.1

⌒ Fiber

Many women find they tend to become constipated in pregnancy, because pregnancy hormones slow movement of the bowel muscles. Constipation can make mothers feel unwell, and may lead to hemorrhoids if you frequently strain to pass stool. It is important to eat foods with plenty of fiber, such as:

◆ Whole-grain bread

◆ Unrefined cereals like granola, or those rich in bran

◆ Raw fruit and vegetables

It's also important to drink plenty of fluids.

⌒ Vitamins

Vitamins are essential in pregnancy, both to keep you healthy and for the development of your baby. Research has shown that mothers who have deficiencies in certain vitamins are at a greater risk of having a baby with disabilities or a baby with a low birth weight. Table 3.1 on pages 50 and 51 shows which vitamins you need and what they do. Remember that taking too much of certain vitamins can be harmful too, so check with your doctor.

Folic acid—a B-group vitamin—has been found to help prevent spina bifida and other neural-tube defects. Studies continue on its benefits during pregnancy. The current recommended dietary allowance for pregnant women is 0.4mg a day. Women who have had a baby with a neural-tube defect are advised to take more, preferably beginning prior to the pregnancy. Check with your doctor.

⌒ Foods to avoid

Recently publicity has been given to a number of foods that may contain micro-organisms that can cause harmful disease in pregnancy. Listeria is an illness caused by a bacteria called *listeria monocytogenes*. Listeria is a mild, flu-like disease in adults, but in a pregnant woman it can cause miscarriage, stillbirth or severe illness in the newborn baby. Listeria can be found in soft cheeses such as Brie, Camembert and blue-veined cheeses, and can also be found in pâtés. Cooked foods that tend to sit out, such as rotisserie chicken, food in buffet lines or deli counters, can also contain low quantities of listeria and must therefore be thoroughly reheated. Salmonella, which can cause acute food poisoning, may be found in undercooked chicken and in raw or soft-boiled eggs, so some women prefer to avoid these. Recent research has shown high levels of vitamin A are concentrated in liver. High amounts of vitamin A can be harmful, so don't overdo eating liver as an iron source.

Toxoplasmosis is another organism that causes only mild symptoms in an adult but that can injure the fetus, causing blindness or hydrocephalus, which can cause brain damage. Toxoplasmosis is found in some raw meat, unpasteurized goat's milk or cheese, unwashed raw fruit and vegetables, and in anything contaminated by cat feces. Someone else will have to empty the cat's litter box while you are pregnant. Also, keep the cat off all counters and tabletops. Wash them off frequently.

Since a pregnancy is not usually confirmed until six or eight weeks after conception, and it may take a little time for the body to build up depleted stores of vitamins and essential minerals, it is very important to adjust your diet *before* you become pregnant if at all possible. A good diet will also make you feel stronger and healthier and help you through the demanding months of pregnancy, through the birth itself and through the postnatal period. If you feel better, you will be more likely to enjoy your baby to the utmost.

⌐ Preconception care

As we learn more about how diet, drugs and other substances in the environment might affect an unborn baby, more and more mothers are trying to prepare well in advance for the birth of their baby. Genetic counselors are available if you know of any genetic disorder in the family or if you are at greater risk of having a baby with disabilities. Advice on diet and general health care in pregnancy may be available at your prenatal clinic or your doctor's office. Talk with your doctor about getting this extra attention if you would like it.

It is worth having your health checked before you conceive.

You might want a Pap smear. You can also have a swab done to check that there are no harmful micro-organisms in the vagina. Recent research shows that thrush and gardnerella, a bacteria that causes bacterial vaginosis, may be linked to a difficulty to conceive, that an organism called *mycoplasma* may be linked to miscarriage, and gardnerella to premature deliveries. Not all such infections cause symptoms normally, but they may cause problems in pregnancy. Checking on them before you're pregnant may be wise.

It is also true that the majority of women do not want to wait months to conceive, and many conceive by accident, or experience problems in conceiving, and these mothers may feel guilty that they are not doing the right thing: "We started out with all the best intentions, stopping smoking and drinking, taking vitamin pills and eating only health-foody things without any additives. But it took me nearly two years to get pregnant. By the end I was fed up with the whole thing—we never enjoyed ourselves, we felt guilty about everything we ate or didn't eat. In the end I just ate what I felt like and let it go at that."

Genetic counseling is available at many hospitals for those who are worried that they may be at extra risk of having a baby with disabilities—this includes older mothers and those who have some hereditary illness or genetic defect in their family.

"We had genetic counseling at the hospital because I was 40 and my husband was too, and his child by his previous marriage had had problems. There was a blockage at the entrance to her stomach. She had to be operated on at birth, but she's fine now. We were told doctors could pick up on this with an ultrasound scan, because the baby would not be able to swallow the amniotic fluid, which otherwise would show up in the stomach. The ultrasound was reassuring. By knowing of any problems in advance, our doctors would be set to do immediate surgery after the baby's birth. I was also concerned about the extra risk of having a baby with Down syndrome—I was surprised at how greatly the risk went up between the ages of 40 and 41. We decided to have the amniocentesis and other tests done because we felt we couldn't have coped with a baby with severe disabilities. I thought the counseling was very helpful and reassuring."

Genetic counseling can be helpful. It enables the couple to talk through any worries they have and to put the risks they are facing into proportion. This is especially true for older mothers who may feel *this* pregnancy is their only chance to have a baby. It can also be helpful in establishing the reasons for any previous babies born with disabilities in the family, or for several miscarriages, and point toward ways of overcoming them. For example, it has been shown that mothers of babies with spina bifida had far fewer affected babies in subsequent pregnancies if they took supplements of vitamin B and folic acid. Some couples who have had several miscarriages have been told this was linked to a genetic problem but that if they kept going they had a chance of having a normal pregnancy, and this has encouraged them to continue trying to conceive.

Keeping fit in pregnancy

Exercise and general physical fitness are very important in pregnancy. Your body changes shape and new stresses and strains are put on it, culminating in the physical stress of the birth itself. By making sure your body is strong and fit you will be helping yourself in pregnancy and working towards an active and safe birth, as well as giving yourself energy and resilience for the demanding time ahead.

During pregnancy your joints tend to loosen slightly; this enables the pelvis to stretch during birth to let the baby through, but it also means you are more likely to strain your ligaments and joints and, especially, your back. Be careful of putting strain on your back by picking things up awkwardly or carrying loads that are too heavy. The weight of your baby in front will make even simple movements like getting out of a chair or a bed potentially damaging for your back, so take care to move in such a way as not to put undue strain on it:

◆ Roll onto your side and push yourself up from there to get out of bed.

◆ Use your legs, not your back, to maneuver yourself up and out of a chair.

◆ When picking up a toddler or a full shopping bag, squat down and then push up with your thighs rather than bending over with your knees straight and lifting from your back.

You can do a number of exercises in pregnancy to keep yourself supple and to strengthen muscles that you will use in the birth itself. However, not everyone is very good at following an exercise program. If you are working or you have other children, it may seem especially hard to fit them in. Gentle walking and especially swimming are good exercises in pregnancy if you enjoy them. You can continue with your usual sports, but gently; remember that if you get out of breath you are depriving your baby of oxygen too. Exercise in pregnancy should be gentle rather than rushed. Don't start an exercise program at this time without checking it out with your doctor first. He will work with you to find an activity that is safe and that you like to do.

Women who want an active labor should practice holding positions such as squatting, standing on all fours or sitting semi-upright to see what position they find most comfortable and to strengthen those muscles they will use.

Be careful of putting strain on your back by picking things up awkwardly or carrying loads that are too heavy.

All women, however, will benefit from locating and exercising the pelvic-floor muscles. (See box, page 57.) These muscles are very important in pregnancy and childbirth. They support the uterus, bowel and bladder. About half of all women who have had children suffer from some weakness in these muscles, with such symptoms as discomfort in the pelvic area or leaking a little urine when they sneeze, cough or lift heavy objects. If these muscles become too weak it can lead to prolapse of the womb (the uterus is displaced downward in the body). You can feel what it is like to use the pelvic-floor muscles by tightening your buttocks and pulling upwards as if you want to empty your bladder but must hold it. The same muscle tightens the vagina and can cause pleasant sensations when you are making love. If you cannot feel the muscles tighten, then try interrupting the flow of urine when you are emptying your bladder; you will soon be able to recognize the sensation.

⌐ Prenatal care

Good prenatal care, as well as taking care of your health and looking after yourself, is the key to a healthy pregnancy. Doctors and other health professionals know it is mainly by improving prenatal care that they can better the health of mothers and babies, and reduce the small number of babies who are born with difficulties and who die. Much of the prenatal care you will receive is routine. It is intended to detect any problems early, so action can be taken to prevent problems from getting worse.

Gentle walking and especially swimming are good exercises in pregnancy if you enjoy them.

Skipping appointments or failing to make use of the services available puts you and your baby at risk. This may be particularly true for the older mother. One study by the World Health Organization (WHO) showed that older mothers (over 35) in countries where they received good prenatal care were at no greater risk during pregnancy and labor than younger women; this was not the case in countries with poor health care during pregnancy.

Kegel Exercises

You can exercise the pelvic-floor muscles unseen every day when you are lying down, standing or sitting. Simply do four to six contractions of about 5 seconds each at various intervals during the day. You can try to do them at the same times each day—when you're brushing your teeth or taking a bath, waiting for the morning bus and so on—to help you incorporate them in your daily routine.

Don't forget to continue with these exercises after the baby is born. Kegel exercises will help strengthen the pelvic-floor muscles after the inevitable stretching they will have undergone during the birth.

ᗡ Finding out you are pregnant

Most women want to know they are pregnant as soon as possible, especially if they have had problems conceiving. Over-the-counter pregnancy tests available now can tell you whether you are pregnant or not as soon as, or even before, your period is due. They are quite accurate. You can buy them at larger grocery stores and at pharmacies. Each box usually contains two tests, so if the first isn't positive, you can repeat it a few days later to make sure. They are not cheap, so it may be wise to wait for your period, and take the test if you are late.

One study by the World Health Organization (WHO) showed that older mothers (over 35) in countries where they received good prenatal care were at no greater risk during pregnancy and labor than younger women.

"When my period was overdue I did a home test and it was positive. Then my doctor did one and it was negative. We were both disappointed. But my period didn't start, and I *felt* pregnant. So I did another home test, which was positive. I called my husband and asked him to come home from work to make sure I wasn't imagining it. He did and agreed it was positive. But the next test from the hospital was negative too—until the doctor called and said they had made an error. It seemed crazy to us that a home test was so much better than the hospital one!"

Having your pregnancy confirmed early lets you, if you haven't already, stop all drinking of alcohol, take care of your diet, and get the soonest possible prenatal appointment. Once you know you are pregnant, talk things over with your healthcare professional and explain any preferences you have for the kind of birth you would like, which hospitals you prefer, whether you would like a hospital delivery or a home birth if that can be arranged. Your doctor will know the options in the area and will be able to discuss with you what is best. In practice this is not always the case, and older mothers in particular may find they are only offered a hospital birth or are under strong pressure to have the baby in the hospital. In some areas, your choice of hospital is limited.

The vast majority of births take place in hospitals, and most people still have their prenatal appointments under an obstetrician's care. Although things seem to have improved in prenatal care, the majority of women find the wait for office appointments is still a problem. There are usually no facilities for occupying the attention of older children and toddlers. In some managed-care systems, women complain that they are seen by someone different each time and may not even see the professional they were supposed to see. Many women find the care impersonal and offhand. But despite these kinds of problems, on the whole, older pregnant women do not find themselves much of an oddity at prenatal clinics.

Over-the-counter pregnancy tests available now can tell you whether you are pregnant as soon as, or even before, your period is due.

"I realized I could be the mother of the woman sitting next to me, but it didn't seem to matter. We were both going through the same thing. I was never once made to feel that I was old or doing anything unusual by the other women or by the office staff. I'd guess the average age of mothers at my clinic was 30 to 35. My doctor does specialize in women with potential difficulties and older mothers, and I live in a major metropolitan area. I think all that makes a difference. Still, I was surprised at the number of older women I saw."

Routine prenatal tests

Ideally, you will have seen your doctor before you conceived, or as soon after conception as possible. At your first appointment, your healthcare provider will take your medical history, together with any details of previous pregnancies. You will be weighed. You are likely to be given an internal examination to confirm the pregnancy, check the womb is the size it should be for your dates, check for any abnormalities of the pelvis and check that the cervix (neck of the womb) is tightly closed. A cervical smear (Pap smear) is also usually taken. Lab tests may be done now or at a later visit.

If you have had a history of miscarriage the doctor may agree not to examine you internally at this stage if you wish, though there is no particular evidence to suggest this might cause a miscarriage.

A blood test is also taken to find your major blood group, particularly whether you are rhesus positive or negative. About 85% of the population is rhesus positive. If you are rhesus negative and your baby is rhesus positive, and it is a second or subsequent pregnancy, there is a small chance that you may make sufficient antibodies to rhesus-positive blood to damage your baby's blood cells. Because of this, if you are rhesus negative, blood samples will be taken at various times throughout your pregnancy to check on antibody levels, which only rarely become too high. Very rarely a baby suffering from rhesus incompatibility may have to be delivered by Cesarean section and receive a blood transfusion.

At every visit you will be weighed to check the growth of the baby and to see that your weight gain is satisfactory.

Rhesus incompatibility is becoming rarer because most rhesus-negative mothers now have an injection of Rh-immune globulin, which prevents them from producing antibodies. If this is done after every delivery or abortion, future babies are safe from rhesus incompatibility.

Your hemoglobin level is checked to make sure you are not anemic (this test will be repeated later in the pregnancy). You are also screened for immunity to rubella (German measles) and for any sexually transmitted diseases.

Your breasts are usually examined at the first visit to check for lumps. They are *not* being checked to see whether you can breast-feed. No matter what size or shape your breasts or nipples are, you should be able to breast-feed successfully. If your nipples are inverted, you will still be able to breast-feed; you may just need a little extra help at first in getting the baby to latch on properly (see page 135).

At every visit you will be weighed to check the growth of the baby and to see that your weight gain is satisfactory. Your urine is tested at every visit—the first time it will be screened for any infection. At every other visit it will be tested for the presence of protein in the urine, which could indicate you have pre-eclampsia (see below) and to check that you are not developing diabetes.

The abdomen is measured at every visit to check that the womb is growing in size according to your dates. After 20 to 24 weeks your baby's heartbeat can be monitored with a stethoscope. Your blood pressure is also measured at every visit, because high blood pressure can indicate a number of problems, including pre-eclampsia. Your ankles and fingers will be checked for puffiness, a sign of water retention.

∽ Pre-eclampsia

Pre-eclampsia, also called *toxemia of pregnancy,* is a disorder of unknown cause. Symptoms include water retention and high blood pressure. If the condition is allowed to progress unchecked, the blood pressure rises further and the mother suffers headaches and even seizures (eclampsia). Pre-eclampsia puts the baby at risk. The baby may not get enough nourishment. Mothers with pre-eclampsia have an increased risk of going into premature labor.

Doctors look carefully for signs of pre-eclampsia or toxemia, because it can be prevented if caught early, and the risk to the unborn baby can be reduced. Although the cause of pre-eclampsia is unknown, it has been linked to poor nutrition in some cases. Older mothers are at greater risk of developing this condition, so it's important to keep all your regular prenatal appointments.

Pre-eclampsia is usually treated with bed rest. Women with this condition are often admitted to the hospital so they and the baby can be monitored. Usually complete rest takes care of the problem. If it does get worse, the baby may have to be born early by Cesarean-section delivery (C-section).

∽ Twin pregnancies

It may come as a surprise to learn that older mothers are more likely to have twins than their younger counterparts. Identical twins are the result of the fertilized egg splitting in two and developing in exactly the same way, since they contain exactly the same genetic material. This occurs at random and does not seem to be influenced by heredity or age. Non-identical (fraternal) twins occur when two eggs are released in a cycle by the ovary, and both are fertilized. Non-identical twins are no more alike than other brothers and sisters. The chance of conceiving fraternal twins increases with age, especially if there are other non-identical twins in the family or if a woman has been taking certain fertility drugs before conceiving.

A twin pregnancy needs special care and monitoring. It puts an extra strain on the body, especially in older mothers. You will need to watch for signs of high blood pressure and anemia and you will need extra rest. Regular, watchful prenatal care is essential. Twin babies are more likely to be born prematurely. Sometimes one baby grows larger than the other, which may be of low birth weight, or both babies may be underweight. The birth will take place in the hospital because the second baby has a higher risk of complications if it is not born soon after the first, especially if it is not in the usual head-down position.

⌒ Emotional changes in pregnancy

It is as important to take care of yourself emotionally in pregnancy as it is to take care of your physical well-being. Emotional self-care can seem much more difficult! Many women find they change a lot in pregnancy: They feel more vulnerable and easily upset. Or they become preoccupied with the new life inside them and find it is more difficult to pay attention at work, visit friends or put energy into making their relationship with their partner run smoothly. Pregnancy thus tests many couples, though potentially it is a very rewarding time for them, too.

For older women, pregnancy and the accompanying loss of physical independence may come as something of a shock. "I was used to being able to control everything," says Pam, 41, "and then suddenly I couldn't. I thought I could do everything just the same but my body told me otherwise! At the beginning it was the tiredness and the nausea. At the end it was that I was just so *big*, and I just couldn't concentrate. And if anything at work went wrong, I felt like bursting into tears. I felt so vulnerable."

Carla became pregnant at 41 after trying for two years. "It never occurred to me that I wouldn't conceive. I assumed if I wanted a baby I could have it like everything else." The pregnancy came at a good time, when Carla was able to take some time off work, which helped her get through the morning sickness and tiredness. "I think my age did make me more tired. I was working hard and trying to prove it didn't make any difference."

A woman's feelings may depend on how well she feels in pregnancy as well as on the closeness of her relationships with her partner, family and friends and, perhaps most important of all, how much the pregnancy was planned and hoped for:

Older women in pregnancy, particularly, may worry about the health of their baby and the birth itself . . . this attitude may depend to some degree on the attitude of the health professionals who care for them in pregnancy.

"I got pregnant by accident—I wasn't too pleased when I got the news! I had a teenage daughter by my first marriage and none in my second, but we'd agreed not to have any. My initial reaction was resentment, and the doctor offered a termination. I woke up and cried every morning to think that I was pregnant. But my husband had had no children in his first marriage. When I sat and thought about an abortion, I couldn't have done it because of him."

"After infertility tests and a miscarriage I was so thrilled to be pregnant! I went around in a daze for the whole pregnancy, despite morning sickness and other discomforts. I couldn't contain myself, it was so exciting."

Some women find work becomes a strain: "I thought pregnancy wouldn't change me. What was I thinking! For the first three months I was terribly, bone-achingly tired. I couldn't concentrate on work. I hate to admit this, but it was true."

Karen had the same experience. "It was difficult, dragging into work those first months with bad morning sickness. I used to throw up regularly in the office bathroom as soon as I got in—it's a miracle I was never sick on the bus! Then, later, I was couldn't concentrate in meetings because the baby was kicking so much. It was odd to be there talking about work plans and schedules while this tremendous thing was going on inside me. I also became very cow-like and contented—I couldn't rush for deadlines any more.

They seemed so unimportant."

Others, perhaps those with less pressure on them, find that they can really relax and enjoy the pregnancy and live it to the full. "I felt great when I was pregnant. I felt fit and healthy and relaxed and let myself be taken care of."

⌣ Prenatal depression

A great deal has been written about *post*natal depression, but very little about *pre*natal depression, although it is certainly common for women to be depressed in some stages of pregnancy. Many women feel overwhelmingly tired. Social engagements, work, housework and relationships all suffer if other people do not understand:

"I used to go to bed whenever I could. The house got really, really messy because I couldn't face cleaning it. I couldn't be bothered to cook nice meals and I didn't have the energy to go to parties or to movies with friends. My husband used to groan because every night about nine o'clock I'd just say, 'I'm exhausted, I'm going to bed now.' A lot of the time I was too tired for sex as well."

Depression is perhaps particularly common in a second pregnancy, especially when the woman has a toddler or young child to care for. No one makes quite the same fuss over you after the first pregnancy, and it is harder to get the extra rest you need. Working women may find the second pregnancy particularly tiring and feel that they are not being efficient at their work, which can contribute to feelings of depression.

Older women in pregnancy, particularly, may worry about the health of their baby and about the birth itself—whether they will have complications and whether there will be anything wrong with the baby. Their attitude may depend to some degree on the attitude of the health professionals who care for them in pregnancy:

"I found out I was pregnant by accident in my early forties, too late to have an abortion or even the tests [tests are dealt with in chapter 4]—my provider was very nervous about it and my husband worried and thought something would be wrong. The scans indicated a different due date and showed the baby was small—it was a scary time.

"I worried about the birth because of my age, but the genetic counselor was fantastic. He said, 'You're a healthy woman—you should have a super-easy birth'—he was very reassuring."

ᐩ Sex in pregnancy

Many couples continue with a happy and fulfilling sex life right through the pregnancy, and doctors today reassure women that sex in pregnancy is perfectly safe and will not harm the baby. There are a few circumstances in which this isn't true: Women who have had a history of miscarriage or threatened miscarriage may be advised to avoid sexual intercourse until after the time when the miscarriage or threat occurred, or until after the first 12 to 16 weeks of pregnancy. Women who have had a premature labor may also be advised to avoid intercourse in the last months, for fear of precipitating labor.

Research has shown that substances called *prostaglandins* found in sperm can help soften the cervix and induce labor, so if your baby is overdue, sexual intercourse can be a good way of getting labor started. In a normal pregnancy, however, there is no evidence that having sexual intercourse or experiencing an orgasm will upset the pregnancy.

Many women find that they get increased pleasure from sex in pregnancy; the increased blood supply to the genital area and the strong contractions of the womb during orgasm can all heighten sensation. Some women feel a particular closeness to their partners during pregnancy that they need to express sexually, and others seek reassurance that they are still desirable.

Not all women feel this way, however. Some feel they need to retreat somewhat into their bodies and concentrate on the baby, and they feel sex intrudes on this. Tiredness and other discomforts at the end of pregnancy may also make some women feel less like having sex, while others may feel that different ways of expressing love and affection are more appropriate. A small study of women's feelings about sex before and after the birth showed that only half the women in the sample were still having sexual intercourse 12 weeks before the birth, so these feelings are certainly normal. Towards the end of pregnancy, sex in the usual positions may become very uncomfortable, so you might experiment with other positions—something many couples find adds spice to their sex life. A lot of women find full penetration very uncomfortable at the end of pregnancy, especially when the baby's head has "engaged" and dropped into the pelvis. At this point, positions that avoid deep penetration are preferable. It is important for women to talk openly to their partners about their wishes and feelings in pregnancy. Otherwise, sex can become a focus for dissatisfaction and resentment.

Problems in pregnancy

Anemia

Women are always prone to an iron deficiency because they lose blood every month through menstruation. If a woman does not have sufficient reserves before pregnancy, anemia may result because of the increased volume of blood circulating through the body. Symptoms of anemia include tiredness, lethargy, irritability and pale skin. Anemia is treated easily with iron supplements.

Diabetes

Women with diabetes run special risks in pregnancy and are usually kept under careful medical supervision. However, today it is perfectly possible for a woman with diabetes to have a normal pregnancy and labor.

Diabetes can be unmasked by pregnancy because pregnancy puts extra strain on the body. Older mothers are more susceptible to this. If diabetes is detected with a urine test, the mother's blood-sugar levels will be monitored. Diabetes may be controlled by diet alone or with insulin injections, the dosage of which may be altered as the pregnancy progresses. Because a woman with diabetes is at risk of having an unusually large baby, birth is sometimes induced early or the mother may be advised to have a Cesarean-section delivery.

Jenny is diabetic and had two children in her thirties. "I knew from the beginning of my first pregnancy that I was going to have a Cesarean. When my first child was born, almost all diabetic women ended up with a Cesarean. It was done with an epidural so I would be awake to see the baby, but the epidural went wrong. I had a headache and had to lie flat on my back for 48 hours after the birth, and I had pain in my legs for about ten days afterwards.

"I waited five years to get pregnant again. I wanted to have the same kind of birth a healthy person does, because that's how I see myself. There was a little scare because the baby was overdue, but when I was one week late I went in, was induced and had a normal, easy birth."

⌒ *Pre-eclampsia*

This is a metabolic disturbance in pregnancy with symptoms of high blood pressure, swelling of the feet, hands and ankles and protein in the urine. It occurs more frequently in older women, but is also linked to obesity and poor nutrition. If untreated, the woman will get headaches, blurred vision and may go on to develop eclampsia, in which she suffers from seizures. The main risk is not to the mother but to the baby, because there is a high risk of premature labor.

Pre-eclampsia is usually treated with bed rest. The mother's blood pressure is watched carefully. If it is late in the pregnancy and her blood pressure goes too high, the baby will typically be delivered early by Cesarean section.

⌒ *Postpartum hemorrhage*

Bleeding before 28 weeks in pregnancy usually results in a miscarriage. After 28 weeks any bleeding is known as *postpartum hemorrhage* and has two main causes: placental abruption, a rare condition in which the placenta separates from the wall of the uterus, and placenta previa. Both conditions are slightly more common in older mothers.

Placenta previa is a condition in which the placenta is attached to the lower part of the womb, near or even over the cervix. This results in bleeding during pregnancy and more bleeding as soon as labor starts. Usually the condition can be identified with an ultrasound scan. Most mothers with placenta previa have to rest in the hospital until the baby is due. This helps prevent bleeding. The baby is delivered by Cesarean section.

⌔ Miscarriage

Miscarriage is a problem of great concern to most older mothers. This risk is particularly disturbing for mothers who have had problems conceiving.

The risk of miscarriage for older mothers is greater than for younger mothers. It is not commonly known that as many as one in six recognized pregnancies end in miscarriage; the numbers would be higher still if all pregnancies were counted, including those that end so soon that a period is only slightly delayed or not delayed at all. There seems to be a slightly higher risk of miscarriage in a first pregnancy.

Miscarriages are even more common for older mothers. One study of women who conceived through artificial insemination by donor showed that by the age of 40 a mother had a 50% chance of having a miscarriage. Studies have shown that about 50% of miscarried fetuses are genetically abnormal. This is why many people try to comfort the woman who has lost her baby with "It's nature's way of getting rid of babies that are not normal." In older mothers, the proportion of fetuses with abnormalities may be higher. New research on helping older women conceive using hormone replacement and donated eggs has shown that it is more likely to be the quality of the embryo than deficiencies in the mother's womb that cause a pregnancy to fail.

The great majority of women who have miscarriages will have a healthy baby eventually.

Having one miscarriage does not mean you have any greater chance of a second. After two miscarriages, the risk does go up, from about one in five to one in three; after three subsequent miscarriages, the chances are about 50/50 that the pregnancy will go to term. But the great majority of women who have miscarriages will have a healthy baby eventually.

Medically, a distinction is made between miscarriages that

occur up to about 12 or 13 weeks and those that occur after this time, because they usually have different causes. The great majority of miscarriages—about 85%—occur before the end of the twelfth week of pregnancy.

What happens when you have a miscarriage?

The first sign of a miscarriage during the first three months of pregnancy is a small amount of bleeding, like the start of a period. Some women say they stop feeling pregnant before this happens—symptoms such as tender breasts or nausea may fade. Spotting may go on for several days and may cease—in which case the pregnancy will continue normally—or it may progress, become heavier. There may be period-like pains or severe cramping. If a woman has some bleeding, this is known as a *threatened miscarriage* or *threatened abortion* (medical terminology does not distinguish between an induced abortion and a miscarriage, which can distress women who overhear doctors using the word "abortion" in a much-wanted pregnancy). If a miscarriage threatens, there is about a 50/50 chance of losing the pregnancy. If the bleeding becomes very severe or if there is a lot of pain, this is usually an *inevitable miscarriage*—either the fetus is dead or the cervix (entrance to the womb) is open and nothing can save the pregnancy.

When a miscarriage occurs after the first three months of pregnancy, it may follow a similar pattern, or it may be very sudden, without much bleeding or pain. A miscarriage may be comparatively quick and painless, or it may involve a long labor. Some doctors may give painkilling injections or even an epidural as in childbirth, but this is rare. Once the miscarriage is over, the woman usually is given a D&C (dilatation and curettage, or scraping of the womb) to make sure that nothing of the pregnancy is left behind that could lead to an infection or hemorrhage, or that could damage the woman's future fertility.

What causes a miscarriage?

In most cases, doctors can't find the cause of an individual miscarriage. Miscarriages are so common that doctors will not investigate unless there are special circumstances, or unless the woman has had three miscarriages or more. In most cases the woman conceives again before too long and has a normal pregnancy.

If the woman does have several miscarriages, and the miscarriages occur at different times in each pregnancy, doctors normally refer to this as *recurrent miscarriage*. Usually recurrent miscarriage is the result of very bad luck. If the miscarriages occur at the same time in each pregnancy and with the same symptoms, the condition is known as *habitual miscarriage* and is usually traced to one medical cause.

Most miscarriages seem to be caused by once-only accidents in the whole complex process of pregnancy. The processes of fertilization, early growth of the embryo, implantation of the fertilized egg into the lining of the womb and the establishment of the right environment for the fetus to develop are all very complicated and delicate. It is not surprising that sometimes things go wrong.

⌒ Blighted ovum

Women who miscarry sometimes hear the term "blighted egg" or "blighted ovum" used to explain what went wrong. This means that either the egg or the sperm that fertilized it were abnormal, so the fertilized egg failed to develop. This will usually result in early miscarriage. Some women who have also had normal pregnancies say that often in such a pregnancy they do not "feel pregnant" even though a pregnancy test is positive.

⌒ Hormonal problems

Another reason for miscarriage may be hormonal problems. This is actually much rarer than was once thought, because today doctors tend to think that a decrease in levels of progesterone, a hormone necessary to sustain a pregnancy, is a symptom and not a cause of failed pregnancy. Some women may have a progesterone deficiency, which is not enough to prevent pregnancy but severe enough to allow a miscarriage to occur. This can usually be established by taking blood samples throughout a woman's monthly cycle and screening these for the level of hormone.

Some women seem to produce too much of the hormone testosterone. Testosterone is usually thought of as a male hormone but women also produce it in smaller quantities. Illnesses such as over- or under-functioning of the thyroid or adrenal glands, or diabetes, can also affect a pregnancy. Acute illness with high fever, such as severe influenza or some rare viral infections, can affect a pregnancy occasionally.

Many miscarriages do seem to occur around the 12-week mark. This is a very delicate time in a pregnancy, when the womb suddenly starts to expand rapidly as the fetus begins to speed up its growth, and when the task of maintaining hormone levels switches from the corpus luteum—the follicle in the ovary from which the egg was released—to the placenta itself. In some cases the hormone levels fall too soon and the pregnancy fails.

In some cases, abnormalities of the womb—such as the presence of fibroids (see page 26)—may cause miscarriages.

◌ *Incompetent cervix*

After 13 weeks, miscarriages are either caused by problems in the attachment of the placenta to the wall of the uterus, or by what is known as an *incompetent cervix*. The muscles around the entrance to the womb are very strong. They have to be if they are expected to hold the growing weight of the fetus and the fluid sac enclosing it. But if the cervix is weak, the cervix may dilate too soon in the pregnancy and cause the bag of waters and the fetus to be expelled. A cervix may be weakened if it has been stretched too much in an earlier pregnancy. It may be weakened during an induced abortion or an operation such as a D&C.

◌ *Moles*

An occasional abnormality of pregnancy that can cause miscarriage is a hydatid mole, which occurs in about one in 2,000 pregnancies. It is more common in older women. In a molar pregnancy, a great deal of placental tissue is formed, but no embryo. The woman often feels sick because of the overproduction of placental hormones. The pregnancy may seem too large for the dates. Usually the mole is miscarried. Sometimes it is identified by an ultrasound scan.

⌇ *Immunological problems*

Some women have repeated miscarriages, sometimes very early in the pregnancy, and seem unable to carry a baby to term. Often this is because the woman or her partner has a chromosomal abnormality, which means these babies would not develop properly. Recently researchers have recognized that some women miscarry because their bodies reject the baby in their womb as a foreign object and expel it. Normally, a complicated mechanism prevents the immune system from rejecting the baby and allows the mother's body to tolerate a "foreign body" in her uterus. In some couples who have similar tissue types this process fails to work properly.

⌇ Preventing miscarriages

Unfortunately little progress has been made in understanding what can be done to prevent miscarriages. Because a high proportion of miscarried fetuses are abnormal, doctors do not want to intervene and prolong a pregnancy where the fetus cannot survive or will be born with severe health problems.

If the cause is an abnormality of the uterus, such as fibroids, surgery can help. If an incompetent cervix is diagnosed, a doctor can stitch together the muscles of the cervix at around 14 weeks before a miscarriage can occur. Then he can remove these stitches a week or two before the baby is due in a simple procedure.

When miscarriage threatens, the usual treatment is bed rest. Some doctors recommend that the woman lie down full-time, getting up only to go to the bathroom. Others believe that she should simply take things very easy. The medical reason for this is, if the placenta is becoming detached, rest may help it become attached more firmly again. In reality, bed rest may not make much of a difference. Usually doctors decide rest "can't do any harm." It is a way of relieving a woman's anxiety by making her feel she is doing everything she can to save the pregnancy. Most women threatening to miscarry instinctively want to rest. However, one study comparing women who rested with another group who couldn't—usually those with other small children to look after—found there was no difference in outcome in the two groups.

This study contradicts other evidence, however. One large study of women who had both planned and unplanned pregnancies showed that while 12% of women with planned, wanted pregnancies had miscarriages, those who had conceived accidentally—all of whom were still using a method of contraception at the time—had twice as many miscarriages. (This does not count women who had IUDs. The rate of miscarriage in women who conceive with an IUD in place is very high—about 60%.)

Researcher Martin Vessey, the professor who conducted this study, calls these results "highly significant." However, no further research has been done as to why more of the unwanted pregnancies failed. There was no question of women trying to interfere with the pregnancy, because all were offered an early, safe legal termination. However, Professor Vessey suggests the women who conceived by accident may have been less "careful" with the pregnancy—perhaps smoking and drinking more, playing strenuous sports or generally "neglecting" the pregnancy.

It is important for women who miscarry to be given information, comfort and reassurance.

The best advice, especially if you have had more than one miscarriage, is to avoid drinking alcohol, smoking, avoiding travel or strenuous activity and stressful situations. You may be advised not to have sexual intercourse until after the time that your previous miscarriage occurred if you are worried about this triggering another miscarriage.

Receiving sympathy and support in a subsequent pregnancy can also help reduce the chance of miscarriage. One study carried out by a British doctor showed that women who were given support and reassurance during their next pregnancies were less likely to have a miscarriage than other women. This shows psychological factors may be at work, and that it is important for women who miscarry to be given information, comfort and reassurance.

ᴄ Coping with a miscarriage

A miscarriage is a very distressing experience; apart from the physical trauma, you have lost the life growing inside you. It can be particularly distressing if you have waited a long time to conceive or if this is a very late baby and you feel you may be running out of time. A miscarriage is a real bereavement, and you should not expect to get over it quickly. It is normally recommended that you wait three months before trying to conceive again, because a pregnancy that occurs very soon after a miscarriage may be more likely to fail again. Women are sometimes advised to wait longer to give themselves time to recover mentally. However, many older women want to begin another pregnancy as soon as possible, especially if they are in their late thirties or their forties. You are bound to be a little nervous in a pregnancy following a miscarriage, but think positive; chances are you will go on to have a healthy baby in the future.

Prenatal Screening

The majority of mothers over the age of 35 who become pregnant can expect a normal pregnancy and a healthy baby. However, older mothers are at greater risk of developing complications. For that reason, an older mother is screened to detect these at an early stage. Older mothers are also at higher risk of having a baby with disabilities, so most are eager to take advantage of the screening tests available.

There can hardly be a mother who has not worried at some time in her pregnancy whether her baby will be normal, and this may be particularly true for the older mother. Fortunately, a number of screening tests are now offered to women at higher risk of having a baby with severe problems. These tests can be very important in easing the parents' worries. In cases where an abnormality is shown, the screening enables them to decide whether or not to proceed with a pregnancy. However, it is important to remember that not all abnormalities can be detected in pregnancy and that accidents at birth can also lead to disabilities. The tests eliminate certain problems but do not guarantee the "perfect baby."

⌐ How the baby develops

A human embryo is more or less completely formed by the end of the twelfth week of pregnancy. After this time it simply has to grow in size and its organs have to mature to make it capable of living outside the womb. All the major developments take place in the early weeks of pregnancy, which is why it is especially important to look after yourself before you even know you are pregnant. The baby's spinal column, for example, begins to form in the fifth week of pregnancy. You are likely at this stage to realize that your period is late, but have not had the pregnancy confirmed. In the sixth week arm and leg buds are formed. In the seventh week the beginnings of the fingers and toes are visible and dramatic changes are occurring to the head and face. In the ninth week the nose and mouth take shape. By the eleventh week the genitals are formed, and all the internal organs are functioning.

Abnormalities in a baby are usually caused by genetic problems or by an environmental influence, such as poor diet, the use of drugs in early pregnancy or by hazards in the workplace, such as toxic chemicals or radiation. Genetic problems fall into two categories: those caused by either or both parents carrying a faulty gene, or those that occur when the sperm or egg are formed. In the second case, the formation involves an extra chromosome or part of a chromosome being included in the fertilized egg.

All the major developments take place in the early weeks of pregnancy, which is why it is especially important to look after yourself before you even know you are pregnant.

⌒ Chromosomes

Chromosomes are the essential components of every living cell. They determine not only how each cell works, but also how the whole organism grows, develops, functions and looks. Chromosomes are made up of smaller units called *genes,* each of which determines a particular characteristic of the organism. Each different animal and plant species has its unique number and size of chromosomes, carrying all the relevant genes. In humans there are 46 chromosomes in 23 pairs. In each individual, one set is inherited from the mother and one set from the father.

When human cells divide to create the sperm or the egg, the pairs of chromosomes are mixed and separated at random so that each egg and each sperm carries a different set of genes, although there will always be one of each chromosomal pair. This is why every human being is different. One of the chromosomal pairs determines the baby's sex. They are called the X *and* Y *chromosomes,* because they look like these letters when viewed under the microscope. When sperm are formed, half carry the Y chromosome, which determines maleness, and half carry the X chromosome. All eggs carry the X chromosome only. It is therefore the father who determines the sex of a baby.

Very occasionally the process of division goes wrong and the sperm or egg cell ends up with an extra chromosome, or sometimes an extra part of a chromosome. When sperm and egg fuse in that case, the embryo will be faulty. In most cases these abnormal sperm, eggs or embryos are not able to survive or, if the embryo does develop, the baby cannot survive long. It is thought that a high proportion—as many as half—of miscarriages are caused by the embryo being abnormal.

Sometimes, however, the presence of an extra chromosome does not prevent the baby from developing or living. The most common instance of this is an extra chromosome on the twenty-first pair of chromosomes, which causes Down syndrome. Other nonfatal chromosomal abnormalities include Turner's syndrome (when a girl lacks an X chromosome), Klinefelter's syndrome (when a boy has an extra X chromosome) or when a boy has an extra Y chromosome.

⌒ Genes

Apart from chromosomal abnormalities, other diseases and disabilities are caused by a faulty gene. Literally hundreds of inherited illnesses are now known, although most are extremely rare. Some of these are caused by a dominant gene, others—and these are more common—by a recessive gene.

A dominant gene is one that will always show itself if it is present, while a recessive gene can remain hidden, perhaps for generations. Each individual inherits one gene for each characteristic from each parent. Suppose the child inherits one gene for blue eyes and one gene for brown. Rather than the two colors being merged, one gene is dominant over the other instead—brown eyes dominate blue, so the individual has brown eyes. However, he still carries a gene for blue eyes which, if it is paired with another gene for blue eyes in his future partner, can express itself in the next generation.

Two relatively well-known, dominantly inherited diseases are Huntington's chorea, a degenerative nerve disease that does not show up till the third or fourth decade of life, and achondroplasia, a form of dwarfism that is linked to older fathers. A person with a dominantly inherited disease has a 50% chance of having an affected child.

Recessively inherited diseases are more insidious because they can be carried by large numbers of people without their knowledge. As long as the recessive gene is only paired with normal genes, there is no problem. However, if two people carrying the abnormal gene have children, their baby has a one-in-four chance of having the disease. Their other children are likely to be carriers.

Recessively inherited diseases include cystic fibrosis, Tay Sachs disease, sickle-cell anemia and phenylketonuria. Some of these can be treated if diagnosed early. Others can be tested for during pregnancy.

Many genes are carried in the X chromosomes and these cause sex-linked diseases if they are abnormal. If a person is female and has two X chromosomes, the abnormal gene is likely to be masked by a normal gene. If it is paired with a Y chromosome, however, there may be no normal gene to mask it, because the Y chromosome is shorter and carries fewer genes. Examples of sex-linked diseases are hemophilia and Duchenne muscular dystrophy.

Some congenital abnormalities (present at birth) are caused not by a simple faulty gene but by a combination of factors. Perhaps several faulty genes are involved, or a combination of a faulty gene with some environmental stimulus, such as a drug taken in pregnancy or an inadequate diet. Neural-tube defects (anencephaly and spina bifida), cleft lip or palate and some congenital heart defects are caused in this way. There may be a random element at work, too. There have been recorded cases of identical twins being born in which one had a cleft lip and the other did not.

Fortunately, most of these problems are relatively rare. But abnormalities such as Down syndrome and spina bifida are more common and more likely to be a cause of concern. On the other hand, these are the abnormalities that tests can detect in the early stages of pregnancy.

⌒ Down syndrome

This is the most common chromosomal abnormality and affects about 1 in 650 live-born infants. The risk of having a baby with Down syndrome increases with the mother's age. At 20, a woman has about a one in 2,000 chance of having an affected child. At the age of 30 the likelihood has risen to about one in 900, and by 40 to about one in 100. After this it rises still more steeply, so that a 43-year-old mother has about a one-in-50 chance and a 47-year-old mother, about a one-in-20 chance. By age 50, the chance is about one in 10. (see Table 4.1). There is also evidence that the risk of having a baby with Down syndrome increases if the father is older than 55.

The most significant problem faced by children with Down syndrome is that they are mentally disabled, although the degree of disability varies. Some can, with help and stimulation, achieve IQs of about 80, considered to be the low end of the normal spectrum; many have IQs of less than 50 and are severely mentally disabled. Children with Down syndrome are also recognized by their flattened profile, slanted eyes with an extra fold and stubby fingers. Most grow slowly and are small for their age. Many have additional disabilities—heart defects, eye abnormalities, hearing problems and a tendency to respiratory infections are common. Babies with Down syndrome are characteristically "floppy" at birth and many have problems with breastfeeding because they may lack the strength to feed properly as well as the reflex to suck.

Most women expect to have a normal, healthy baby when they go into labor, although a very small number may know that their baby is likely to be born with disabilities. When things go wrong and a woman has to face this at the time of the birth, the shock and disbelief can be devastating.

"They told us after the birth that she wasn't normal. I refused to listen. I said, 'If you're worried about her slanting eyes, my

Chromosome Risks by Maternal Age
at term delivery

Maternal age	Down-syndrome risk	Chromosomal-abnormalities risk
20-21	1/1,167	1/526
22-23	1/1,429	1/500
24-25	1/1,250	1/476
26	1/1,176	1/476
27	1/1,111	1/455
28	1/1,053	1/435
29	1/1,000	1/417
30	1/952	1/385
31	1/909	1/385
32	1/769	1/322
33	1/602	1/286
34	1/485	1/238
35	1/378	1/192
36	1/289	1/156
37	1/224	1/127
38	1/173	1/102
39	1/136	1/84
40	1/106	1/66
41	1/82	1/53
42	1/63	1/42
43	1/49	1/33
44	1/38	1/26
45	1/30	1/21
46	1/23	1/16
47	1/18	1/13
48	1/14	1/10
49	1/11	1/8

Table 4.1

Graph 4.1

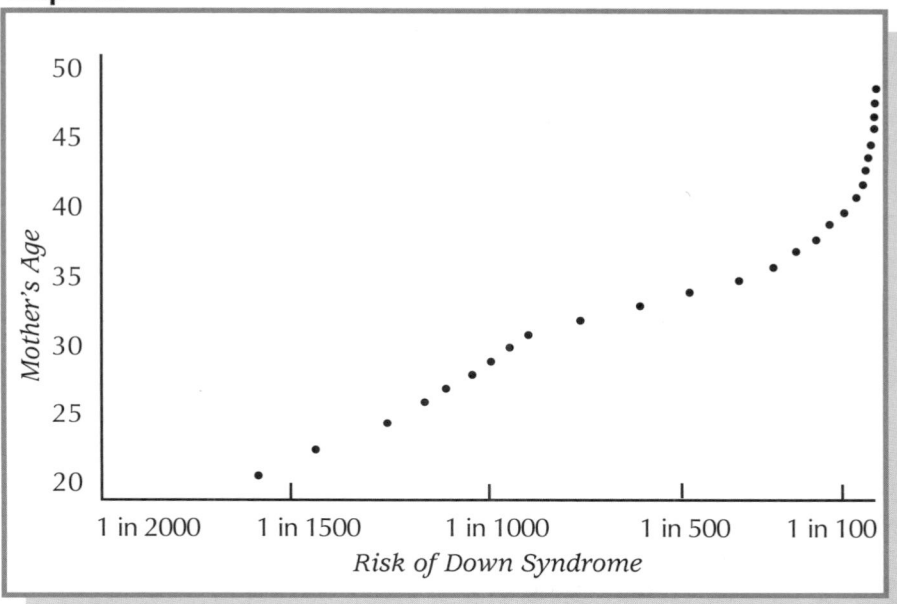

other children had that. They're my husband's eyes.' Then they showed me how she didn't have normal reflexes and how floppy she was and one or two other things, and I had to believe it was true. My husband was also told, and he didn't know what to say; we couldn't look at one another. My first feeling for the baby was absolute hate: I hated her for not being normal. I seriously thought of giving her up for adoption. That feeling lasted a day or two."

It may take the parents days, weeks and sometimes even months to accept what has happened and to acknowledge that a baby born with some form of disability needs just as much love and care as a normal baby.

"I wouldn't talk to the other mothers, or the staff, wouldn't see my family and wouldn't see the baby. Then I thought, she can't be that bad, I'll just go look at her. She was asleep. The nurses had been feeding her. I just looked and looked at her and she was so tiny, so beautiful, like my other babies had been. I felt a rush of love and when my husband came I was feeding her and crying. I told him, 'We have to keep her, she needs us more than anyone.' He just smiled and smiled and said, 'That's what I've been waiting to hear. It doesn't matter, we'll love her anyway.' I won't say things have been easy, but I don't regret having her now, although of course sometimes I wish she had been normal."

Down syndrome is the most common chromosomal abnormality involving an extra chromosome—chromosome 21, in this case. There are others, such as Edward's syndrome, or trisomy 18, involving an extra eighteenth chromosome. Edward's syndrome is the most common trisomy after Down syndrome, and occurs in about one in 5,000 live births. It leads to multiple congenital disabilities and most children die within a few days or weeks after birth, despite medical intervention. Edward's syndrome babies are usually small, with tiny features and pixie-like ears, and have internal heart and kidney abnormalities. As with other chromosomal abnormalities of this kind, there is some association with maternal age.

⁓ Neural-tube defects

Neural-tube defects, which include spina bifida and anencephaly, occur in about three in every 1,000 live births. There is no evidence these problems appear more commonly in the babies of older mothers. Early in pregnancy, a groove appears down the baby's back and this develops into the brain and spinal cord. Normally the groove closes into a tube in which the spinal cord and brain develop, but in rare cases the tube does not close properly. If the defect is in the part of the tube that forms the brain, anencephaly results. This development is always fatal because the upper skull and brain do not form. If the defect occurs lower than around the brain, then part of the spinal cord and nerves protrude, covered by a fragile membrane; the baby is usually paralyzed from this site down. Sometimes, however, spina bifida can be less severe, is not noticeable from outside and results in minimal disability.

As many as 85% of babies severely affected with spina bifida also have a defect called *hydrocephalus*. Cerebro-spinal fluid accumulates in the head, causing mental retardation if untreated. Today the fluid can be drained after birth. Surgery can repair the opening in the spine to reduce the risk of infection. Surgery and other techniques have improved the outlook for children suffering from this disability.

Spina bifida can probably be largely prevented by an adequate diet before and during early pregnancy. Evidence has shown that taking vitamin supplements rich in B-group vitamins and folic acid has greatly reduced the incidence of spina bifida, even in mothers at greater risk because the disability is in their family.

⌒ *Cleft lip and palate*

This is one of the most common abnormalities, affecting about one in 1,000 babies. This is another condition that does *not* seem to be more common in the babies of older mothers. The cleft is caused when the tissues that move together to form the face in very early pregnancy do not fuse, leaving a gap that can involve the lip alone, the palate, or both. The cleft can be on one or both sides of the face and varies in its seriousness. The vast majority of children with cleft lip or palate are fine in other respects, but sometimes another abnormality is present also.

Cleft palate can cause serious feeding problems in the early months, because the baby is unlikely to be able to suck well. The child will have difficulties speaking. Teeth are likely to be missing or malformed in the area of the cleft. Plastic surgery, however, can completely repair the cleft, inside and out, by the time the child reaches maturity. Speech therapy and orthodontic work are usually necessary.

Although cleft lip and palate are correctable, it is understandably distressing to give birth to an affected child:

"Our son was born with a double cleft palate and lip. When he was born it was badly disfiguring, because the middle of his upper lip and jaw were pushed forward, sort of like a beak. He had terrible feeding problems. He couldn't suck and had to be fed with a spoon at first. You can imagine how difficult this is with a hungry, crying baby whose every instinct is to suck! He had to have a series of operations throughout his childhood. The end result is very good. But the emotional effects of hospital stays and of looking different to other children are harder to deal with than the physical repairs."

⌒ *Abnormalities in the digestive tract*

Abnormalities in the digestive tract are other relatively common and correctable defects. They are not normally related to maternal age. These include a blockage of the entrance to the stomach, often accompanied by a situation in which the windpipe and esophagus are joined; and blockages at various points in the digestive tract, including the anus. All are easily corrected by surgery. Some can even be detected in the womb by ultrasound.

⌒ Detecting abnormalities

Some tests are now available to screen all pregnant women. Others are available for women who are at higher risk of having a child with disabilities. Some of these tests are offered to women routinely. Others are offered only to women over a certain age who are already known to be at risk either because of family history or because of previous difficulties with pregnancies. Your healthcare professionals will explain at one of your early prenatal appointments what their procedure is and which tests they offer to women. If they don't, and you would like to know, ask which tests they offer and when during the pregnancy they are performed.

Screening tests include:

◆ Ultrasound scans, which may be used as needed, from the fifth week of pregnancy to delivery

◆ A blood test that can detect raised levels of a substance called *alpha-fetoprotein* in the blood, which may indicate a neural-tube defect

◆ Amniocentesis (a sample of the waters surrounding the baby) enables chromosomes to be examined, shows any chromosomal abnormality and, incidentally, the child's sex

◆ Rarer techniques, such as fetoscopy, in which the baby is examined through a tube inserted into the womb

◆ Chorionic villi sampling, a technique that one day may replace amniocentesis

ᗢ Ultrasound

Since the 1970s, remarkable improvements in ultrasound technology have opened a real "window on the womb." Ultrasound consists of high-frequency sound waves that are bounced off the baby to give a photographic picture of the fetus. Unlike X-rays, which have much higher powers of penetration, ultrasound will identify soft tissues. Thus, it can give a complete picture of the growing baby and is a very useful diagnostic tool.

An ultrasound scan may be used to date the pregnancy, and thereafter used as needed in hospitals with the equipment. If not, women who may be at special risk because of problems with a previous pregnancy, or who would like to have a scan, can often be referred to a hospital where it can be performed. The pregnancy can be very accurately dated at around 16 weeks by measuring the circumference of the baby's head. This knowledge is useful in avoiding problems later if the mother is unsure of her dates and does not know when the baby is due. The scan can locate the position of the placenta, which can be helpful if there is any bleeding later in pregnancy, and it can be used to check that the baby has no major physical abnormalities such as anencephaly. Ultrasound can show congenital heart defects, kidney disease and other severe abnormalities. Ultrasound can also detect if the mother is expecting more than one baby.

All indications are that the benefits of having ultrasound outweigh any potential risk.

There has been some controversy about the safety of ultrasound, which has concerned some women. They are not sure whether they should accept a scan. Ultrasound has now been in use for many years without any evidence of harmful effects to the baby.

All indications are that the benefits of having ultrasound outweigh any potential risk. Not least is the benefit of reassurance given to many women on seeing their baby is alive and well, particularly those who have waited a long time to have a baby or who have experienced a miscarriage. However, a large study carried out in the United States by the National Institutes of Health on 15,000 women with a low risk of problems in pregnancy showed that while detection of twins and malformations was increased, and pregnancy could be dated more accurately, the outcome—in terms of healthy babies—was not improved when ultrasound was employed. There was no difference in the rate of fetal or neonatal death or subsequent illness. Rates for preterm births, for the outcomes of postdate pregnancies and for low-birth-weight babies were similar for those who had had ultrasound and those who had not. Although the percentage of abnormal fetuses detected in the group who had ultrasound was three times higher, the termination rate was about the same in both groups.

So, while ultrasound is of undoubted benefit to women at high risk or in special situations where a problem is detected, its routine benefits are unproved for now. Ultrasound can help some mothers anxious about their pregnancies by reassuring them, but can also create anxieties for others:

"Towards the end of my pregnancy they started to worry about whether my baby was growing as he should. I don't know what started it, but once they got this idea into their heads they wouldn't leave me alone. I was in and out of the hospital having my blood pressure taken and having ultrasound scan after scan. My blood pressure was up—with worry, no doubt—and they couldn't decide what to do. They said they would have to induce the baby early to make sure that all would be well. Then they changed their minds and decided to wait. I was in the hospital for the last few weeks of the pregnancy and, of course, the baby decided to be late. I was two weeks overdue before they decided induce the birth. By then I was so desperate I said, 'Yes.' It was a terrible birth, ending with an emergency Cesarean, and when he was born he was 7 pounds, 1 ounce. He didn't look overdue. I asked my doctor later, 'So what happened with this small baby?' There was nothing wrong at all! My worries were for nothing. They said they couldn't explain it but he had appeared small on the scan. So much for all their wonderful technology!"

Some women—and doctors and midwives, too—feel that,

with the increased reliance on new technology, many of the old skills in obstetrics are being lost:

"I had shared care and I noticed a tremendous difference between my visits to the well-baby clinic and my visits to my very experienced doctor. At the clinic, people seemed to poke and probe for a long time and suggested that I have another scan to see the baby was growing OK. When I went to my doctor, she examined me very quickly and said, 'Oh, this baby's doing fine, I think he weighs about 4 pounds now.' I asked how she knew and she just said, 'Experience.' In the clinic, I feel like you only see the junior staff, with the senior staff called for special occasions. No wonder you don't always get the best care and they give you all kinds of unnecessary tests!"

∼ Having an ultrasound scan

An ultrasound scan is a simple, noninvasive procedure. In early pregnancy you are usually asked to drink a lot of water an hour or two before your appointment and not to empty your bladder. This pushes the womb up in the pelvis and will give the ultrasound operator a clearer view. You will be asked to lie down on a couch and remove any clothing that covers your abdomen. A cold gel is rubbed over the abdomen to enable the ultrasound operator to move the scanner smoothly over the area. As she does so you will see the baby's outline appear on the television screen and you will also see the fetal movements.

It can be difficult to interpret what you are seeing, so ask if you are not told. The operator can freeze the picture at any time and point out things to you without exposing the baby to any more sound waves than necessary. You will usually be able to see the baby's head, the arms and legs moving around, and some of the internal organs at work. You may even be able to see the baby sucking his thumb.

"The woman took a lot of time to explain to me what she was looking for and what she could see. I found all of it so reassuring. She pointed out the heart beating, the cord and the placenta, the kidneys and the spine and showed me how much he was moving around."

Other women find the process unnerving, especially if nothing is explained.

"No one said anything to me and I was afraid to ask in case anything was wrong. She kept on looking at everything and taking measurements and I started to get very jumpy. Then she suddenly got up and said, 'I just want to get a second opinion on this,' and I was terrified. I thought, 'This is it. Something's really wrong.' I was in tears. Someone else came back and they were both looking at the screen, still not saying anything to me. 'What is it, what is wrong?' I finally asked. 'Nothing's wrong, I'm just checking these measurements,' she said. I felt as if I weren't a person—just a scientific toy."

Usually the baby's father is welcome to come and watch the process and see the baby on the screen. Many dads find this is a very positive experience, not only because they are able to give support, but also because the baby becomes real to them in an even more dramatic way than to the woman: "It was hard for me to take in that she was pregnant until I saw the baby on the screen. It was fantastic—it made it come alive for me."

⌣ Alpha-fetoprotein blood test

This is a routine blood test carried out at between 16 and 18 weeks of pregnancy. It measures the level of a substance called *alpha-fetoprotein* (AFP), which gets into the mother's bloodstream from the baby. A high level of alpha-fetoprotein can mean a number of things: that the pregnancy is further advanced than was thought, that the mother is expecting twins, or that the baby is suffering from a neural-tube defect. It can also mean nothing at all!

If a woman does have a higher-than-normal level of AFP, a second blood test will be done to confirm it. If this test is positive also, there is a roughly 1-in-7 chance the fetus has a neural-tube defect. It is usually recommended that the woman have an ultrasound scan to check for the presence of anencephaly or spina bifida. If results are inconclusive, an amniocentesis is usually recommended so that the level of AFP in the amniotic fluid can be measured (see section below).

The problem with the AFP blood test is that for every ten women with a raised AFP level, only one will have a cause found for it. The other nine will have a normal baby, although they may have a slightly greater risk of having a small-for-dates baby. The majority of women with a high AFP level will have a "positive" result and then an amniocentesis performed, accompanied by a lot of stress and worry, when there is actually nothing wrong with their baby. The chance of the AFP level being high from other causes is greater than the risk of a neural-tube defect.

> *The problem with the AFP blood test is that for every ten women with a raised AFP level, only one will have a cause found for it. The other nine will have a normal baby.*

Rather than perform the AFP test routinely without fully consulting the mother, healthcare professionals might do better to explain what the test is for, what it involves, and let the mother choose whether to have it. Some people welcome the test, but others prefer to do without it.

"I had just had the scan, seen the baby moving [and] that its head was there and it was kicking its legs. I thought we would have seen if there was anything really wrong. Its head would have been the wrong shape or its legs paralyzed. Anyway, I couldn't possibly have aborted that baby once I had seen him like that. So I decided not to have the test. What was the point of having it done when I could see there was nothing so wrong with the baby and I wouldn't have wanted an abortion anyway?"

Besides, not all neural-tube defects are detected by the test. There is no absolute level of AFP in the amniotic fluid at which one can say, "This baby is affected and this one isn't." An artificial line has to be drawn. If the level is set too high, more neural-tube defects will go undetected. If it is too low, more women will have further tests with all the worry that goes with it.

A new test known as the *triple-screen test* has been developed. A blood test is taken at 16 weeks and levels of alpha-fetoprotein are measured, together with two other "markers," unconjugated estriol and human chorionic gonadotropin (HCG). High levels of AFP may indicate higher likelihood of a baby with spina bifida, while low levels of AFP and unconjugated estriol, together with high levels of HCG, indicate a higher risk of having a baby with Down syndrome.

Results from the test are combined with the woman's age to give her a "risk factor." A risk of one in 250 or higher is considered "screen positive"—that is, an amniocentesis or further screening is advised. A risk of less than one in 250 is considered "screen negative." However, a positive result means, on average, only a 1-in-50 chance of the woman having a baby with Down syndrome. Again, some experts are concerned that this test will put too many women under great stress who don't need to be by receiving a "positive" test result and having an amniocentesis.

In a more refined version of the test, called the *quad-screen test,* a fourth marker is measured in the blood, neutrophil alkaline phosphatase. This makes the test even more accurate at determining whether or not a fetus may have Down syndrome.

⌒ Amniocentesis

Amniocentesis consists of taking a sample of amniotic fluid in the sac surrounding the baby and analyzing it. Amniotic fluid contains some of the baby's cells, which can be cultured to reveal any chromosomal abnormalities. Amniocentesis can also be used to detect neural-tube defects, because there will be a very high level of AFP in the amniotic fluid in that case. This is much more accurate than the AFP blood test.

Amniocentesis is usually offered to women 35 or older, although the policy may change in the future. Age 35 was chosen originally because at this point it was believed that the risk of potential chromosomal problems with the baby was about the same as the risk of miscarrying the baby as a result of the amniocentesis test. However, amniocentesis is even safer now, so the mother's age at which the test is recommended is being reconsidered upward.

The risk of miscarriage attached to amniocentesis is small. Studies used to quote a rate of about 0.5%, but today it is closer to 0.3%. Some doctors dispute whether there is a real risk at all.

However, for older mothers, especially those with a history of miscarriage or infertility and for whom a pregnancy is particularly precious, there is a real fear of inducing a miscarriage. This can make the decision to have an amniocentesis very difficult.

Cindy was unlucky and had a miscarriage a week after her amniocentesis at the age of 39. "I was devastated. I blamed myself. They had told me the risk but it seemed so small. I'd never heard of anyone actually losing a baby. They said it might not have been the amnio, that it might have happened anyway. But [the amniocentesis] seemed to me to be the most likely reason, because there was nothing wrong with the baby. It was a girl, and I had wanted a girl. I felt I had gone against nature and been punished. It was a terrible, terrible time for me.

"I did get pregnant again a year later and I had a boy. I decided against an amnio and he is fine. Everything is fine, but now I'm 41 and I may not get pregnant again. If I do, now I don't know whether to have an amnio or not. I keep thinking that if I hadn't had one I could now have had two children and my family would be complete. On the other hand, perhaps I should just count myself lucky that I am now a mother and have a healthy child."

An amniocentesis is usually carried out at about 16 weeks into the pregnancy. This is about the earliest time that sufficient amniotic fluid can be withdrawn for testing. Usually an ultrasound scan will also be done at this time, to help the doctor locate the fetus and to identify the best place from which to draw the fluid. You will be asked to have a full bladder for the ultrasound scan, and then asked to empty your bladder before the amniocentesis is performed.

You will change into an examination gown, and the area on the abdomen where the needle is inserted will be swabbed with antiseptic. The needle is usually inserted without local anesthetic. The doctor directs the needle into the amniotic fluid and takes a small amount of the pale-yellow fluid. When ultrasound is used as well, the danger of the needle hitting the baby or placenta is very small. Most women do not find the procedure painful. They describe a slight cramp or pressure in the womb as the needle passes through the uterine wall. Some women feel a little sore for a day or two afterwards. You are usually advised to take it easy because of the slight risk of miscarriage.

For some women, however, the test is not so straightforward:

"We went along [with it] at 16 or 17 weeks. My husband came and we were all keyed up. They did the scan first and said the baby was lying all spread-out and there were no big pockets of fluid to get the needle into, so it wasn't worth trying. We had to go back the following week—the anticlimax was awful."

"While pregnant with Josh at the age of 35, I did worry a lot that he might have disabilities. I was feeling very aware of my age. When I was pregnant with Douglas at 37 I said I wanted an amnio. I was told the risk of this causing a miscarriage was about the same as the risk of the baby having Down syndrome and that I should only consider the test if I was prepared to have an abortion.

"I felt I couldn't handle having a child with disabilities and that it wouldn't be fair to the two boys. I had baby-sat for a child with mental disabilities and I had no illusions about how difficult it was and how it had affected her brother. I would certainly have had a termination if anything had been wrong.

"They made light of the procedure, said I didn't need someone with me, it wouldn't take long and it wouldn't hurt. I was 16 weeks pregnant. Allen drove me to the hospital and waited outside. I was not given an anesthetic. Ultrasound was used to locate the baby and the bag of fluid. An enormous-looking needle was stuck into my very tender belly and it was excruciatingly painful. I gripped the nurse's hand and counted to 60; the nurse kept saying, 'It doesn't usually hurt.' Then it was all over. I was shaking and very distressed. Allen had to help me into the car; there is no way I could have gotten home by myself. I started having contractions when I got home and these lasted for four hours, but I didn't bleed. I thought, 'Oh God, what have I done? I'm going to lose the baby.' I had to stay in bed all day and took things easy the next day.

"Waiting was OK for the first three weeks. Then the results were late, more than four weeks, so I thought something had to be wrong. I started to get very depressed. Although they said they would only tell the mother the results, I couldn't face calling myself and got Allen to phone from his office. They told him all was well and we were both thrilled, though my mother burst into tears when I told her it was another boy. The whole thing was horrible, but it was still better than another four months of worrying. Now I could look forward to the baby happily."

Others find the process much easier than they had thought:

"It was simple. I felt *nothing*. My husband was there and he said, 'Did you really not feel anything? They seemed to take a ton of fluid!' Everyone was extremely helpful and reassuring. It was much, much easier than I had imagined it would be."

Once the test is completed, the drawn fluid is analyzed. Cells in the fluid are cultured and grown over a couple of weeks. Then they are crushed and put under a microscope so the chromosomes can be examined. Very occasionally the test fails and has to be repeated two or three weeks further into the pregnancy:

"*W*e had asked to know the sex of the baby, but they were reluctant to tell us."

"I had an amnio at 16 weeks after much thought and consultation. The first one didn't take, and I had another at 20 weeks, by which time I had felt the baby moving. I couldn't understand what was wrong with the first test. I was worried it meant something was wrong with the baby."

The fluid is also tested for high levels of alpha-fetoprotein, which can indicate the presence of a neural-tube defect.

If you are the possible carrier of a genetic disease, tests can be carried out to identify up to almost 80 hereditary diseases. These tests are time-consuming and expensive, so they will only be done if your family has a history of an inherited illness that technicians can test for.

Waiting for the results can be the hardest part of the whole procedure. Usually women are told the results will take three weeks, though sometimes they are received sooner and rarely, later:

"They said the results would take three weeks but it only took two. They had tried to call but we were out, so they wrote us a very nice letter saying all was well."

You are usually informed by letter or by telephone; you can telephone yourself if the results are overdue. You can also ask to know the sex of the baby if you want to, though some hospitals insist on talking this over with you first:

"We had asked to know the sex of the baby but they were reluctant to tell us. They said to go home and think about it, and asked probing questions about did we want a girl or boy. When they called to say the results were fine, they didn't volunteer the information. We pressed for it and were told it was a girl. We didn't really care about the sex, but we both had a slight preference for a girl. We were delighted and it was wonderful to know, which I hadn't in my earlier pregnancies. In fact, knowing was one of the most important parts of the pregnancy."

Occasionally one partner wants to know the sex and the other doesn't; this is hard to deal with.

There is some evidence that people who desperately want either a son or daughter have problems adjusting to the baby if they know in advance that it is the "wrong" sex. In the heat of the birth itself, most parents are so pleased to know the baby is all right that they don't think much about its sex. The baby is there to love and care for. Knowing this fact while pregnant, however, gives a parent time to brood over the as-yet unknown person and sometimes to reject the baby, making it more difficult to adjust when the baby arrives.

This is an individual matter of course and people have different attitudes about it:

"I wanted to know. I thought if it was there in my notes and other people knew, then of course *I* had the right to know."

"I told them, 'Don't tell me!' I didn't want to know—it would have ruined everything, like unwrapping a present before your birthday."

"If it's a first baby, I think once you know you feel a little sad no matter what, because you want both—you can't really decide which is your preference. So when they said it's a girl, I felt sad in a way that it wasn't a boy. But it wasn't that I actually had *wanted* a boy."

Most hospitals respect people's wishes in the matter, but some provide limited counseling to help a couple decide if they want to know or not. Occasionally one partner wants to know the sex and the other doesn't; this is hard to deal with. If one partner is told and hides it from the other, it puts considerable strain on a relationship at a time when a couple should be as close and open with one another as possible.

Fetoscopy

This technique involves passing a very small tube containing a light and a lens into the uterus so the developing baby can be seen. The tube is introduced through a small incision made just above the pubic bone under a local anesthetic. Fetoscopy is carried out in the second three months of pregnancy. Samples of the baby's blood, skin and liver can be taken. A number of abnormalities can be detected by fetoscopy that cannot be learned any other way. The procedure has recently been used to "operate" on the unborn baby, enabling drugs and transfusions to be put directly into the baby's bloodstream.

The baby is usually viewed at around 16 weeks and blood samples taken between 17 and 22 weeks. External defects (to the face or limbs) and neural-tube defects are clearly visible. Hemophilia and other blood disorders can be detected; so can some diseases of metabolism. The technique is not used lightly, however, because it carries a substantially increased risk of miscarriage, death of the baby in the womb or premature labor.

Chorionic villi sampling (CVS)

This is a relatively new technique being offered in some hospitals as an alternative to amniocentesis. The advantage of the test is that it can be carried out much earlier than amniocentesis. CVS gives the mother who finds that her baby has serious birth defects the chance to terminate the pregnancy earlier, when it can be carried out simply, rather than as induced labor after she has felt the baby moving.

The CVS test is carried out by passing a thin tube through the cervix (neck of the womb) and removing a tiny fragment of tissue from the placenta. This can be done without an anesthetic and, as with amniocentesis, ultrasound is used to show the exact position of the fetus and placenta. The vagina is cleaned with antiseptic solution beforehand to prevent germs from being introduced into the womb.

The test is usually not painful, but it is uncomfortable for many women, a little like having a Pap smear or, some women say, like having an IUD (intrauterine device) fitted. The test takes 10 to 20 minutes and you will be allowed to go home after about an hour. As with amniocentesis, you may be advised to take things easy for a day or two because of the risk of miscarriage. At the moment, this risk seems to be about one in 50, two or three times more likely than with amniocentesis. At present, the test is performed in medical centers. Going to a medical center with a good track record for giving these tests may help reduce the associated risks.

The results can be available quickly, sometimes in a matter of days.

CVS detects chromosomal abnormalities in the same way amniocentesis does, but it does not identify neural-tube defects. Women who have this test will also be given the AFP blood test to detect spina bifida. The results can be available quickly, sometimes in a matter of days.

ᕗ When an abnormality is found

The vast majority of women who have these screening tests in pregnancy are reassured that all is well, and this enables them, and older mothers in particular, to relax and enjoy the rest of their pregnancy. But tests do not detect all problems, and tests are not foolproof. In addition, problems can occur at birth, which can result in a disability.

In the small number of cases where an abnormality is found, however, the pregnancy is transformed from a happy event into a nightmare. Some women feel this is just as traumatic as losing a full-term baby. Knowing you are carrying a child with disabilities and having to decide whether or not to have a termination is one of the most difficult experiences anyone can face. Hospitals often lack adequate support services and do not know how to deal with a couple's distress and grief. A number of organizations can help;

one with a wide network is SHARE (see Useful Addresses, page 172).

Doctors may fail to explain the news well, or there may be confusion over the results:

"They called and said the baby was a girl, and there was a problem. She mentioned Down syndrome, and my thoughts went into a tailspin. She gave me an appointment to see the doctor. I walked around in a daze; I couldn't bring myself to tell anyone. When I saw the consultant, she explained that my daughter would not suffer from Down syndrome herself, but one chromosome was abnormal, so any children she had would suffer from Down syndrome. In other words, the baby I had for days been considering aborting would be perfectly normal."

Another mother felt that the way the news was broken to her was far from satisfactory:

"They didn't call with the results of the amnio so finally I called them. They said, 'Oh, yes, but we can't discuss this over the phone. You have to make an appointment to come in.' I knew then something was wrong, so I asked, 'What is it? Is it Down syndrome?' She said no, it wasn't, and I would have to wait till I saw the doctor. We had to wait another day. They told us there was a high level of alpha-fetoprotein in the fluid and that it was likely the baby had spina bifida. They would like to do another scan to check because they hadn't picked it up before. This time they did. They all looked at the screen, not me, although there were tears pouring down my face

Hospitals often lack adequate support services and do not know how to deal with a couple's distress and grief.

the whole time. The consultant explained what the outlook was and painted this dismal picture for the child. We decided on an abortion right then, but for some bureaucratic reason had to wait. In the meantime I was given no support."

A study carried out in the United States by the National Institutes for Child Health showed that of parents who discover their baby is abnormal, 95% decide on a termination. Some hospitals advise that if a couple knows they do not want to have a termination they should not have the tests, to spare them "unnecessary" expense. However, not all couples know until the decision is upon them. Others feel they have the right to know, no matter what, so they can prepare themselves—both in a practical sense and from an emotional point of view:

"I was 40 and had had years of infertility problems. In fact, a couple of months before I *did* conceive I had been told I would *never* conceive. We discussed the possibility of a child with disabilities and decided to have an amnio, because we didn't want to cope with a baby with severe problems. Before the scan we had decided on a termination if anything was wrong. But when we actually saw the baby, we both came out and said, 'This is it, we won't have a termination.' But we still went ahead and had the amnio."

"We would never have had a termination; I don't believe it's right. But if it had been Down syndrome or something, I would have wanted to know so we could prepare ourselves, read up about it, tell the family in advance. I don't see why that should be kept from you."

It is a particularly harrowing experience if the mother is carrying a sex-linked genetic disease that affects only boys, such as hemophilia or Duchenne muscular dystrophy. The latter is a particularly distressing disease in which a child who appears normal at birth suffers a gradual loss of muscular strength, becomes progressively paralyzed and dies at about the age of 20. If the mother is known to carry the disease, her male offspring has a 50% chance of having the disease. Amniocentesis can tell the parents the child's sex, but not whether he has the disease, so parents can be faced with the agonizing choice of terminating the pregnancy if they are carrying a boy without knowing if he is affected or not. A girl has a 50% chance of being a carrier, but will not have the disease.

IVF has opened up a new possibility for people carrying genetic diseases with pre-implantation diagnosis. Here the woman's ovaries would be stimulated to produce several eggs, which are collected and fertilized "in vitro." About three days after fertilization, one cell can be removed from each embryo and tested for presence of the faulty gene. Only normal embryos would be reimplanted and the woman would have the hope of a pregnancy in which she didn't have to worry about carrying an affected child. However, she would have to go through the full IVF procedure. So far, about 10 pregnancies have been achieved world-wide following pre-implantation diagnosis.

⌐ Problems with screening

Because of these tests, many women enjoy their pregnancy free of certain worries. But for many others, the tests present some very difficult choices. Some women feel they can only start a pregnancy in later life because they have the option of learning if the baby has chromosomal abnormality. Others feel uncertain about this "advantage:"

"We agreed we couldn't cope with a baby with severe disabilities, so I had all the tests. But I don't think having the tests influenced my decision to have a baby. Having a baby is a very emotional decision. I was glad to have the tests but I didn't really think about it in advance—I would have taken the risk."

Other mothers regret the existence of such tests, because they feel it puts an extra strain on the pregnancy:

"Because I was 38 when my first baby was conceived, I decided I would have the amniocentesis done. This turned the first six months of my pregnancy, a time that should have been a happy one for me, into a nightmare.

"First I refused to 'bond' with the baby in my mind, in case there was something wrong with him or her. By the time the test was to be done, I'd worked myself into a state about it, and convinced myself the result would be bad.

"When the test was done I felt contractions, as if I were starting labor, which terrified me. Later I had a threatened miscarriage, which I'm sure was connected. I heard results sooner than I expected, but it was neither a positive nor a negative result, because the test hadn't taken. I was told there was just enough time to repeat the test if I wanted to. After a lot of agonizing I decided to do this.

"*I* don't think the tests being available influenced my decision to have a baby . . . I was glad to have the tests but I didn't really think about it in advance — I would have taken the risk."

"Again I had to wait two weeks—in fact a little longer—before the result came. Everything was fine. I was so relieved! But the whole episode made me feel very protective toward my baby, not wanting him to be interfered with—and at the same time, alienated all that time from him in case he was abnormal."

Because amniocentesis is normally carried out at 16 to 18 weeks, and the results take from two to four weeks to come back, a woman can be as far along as 22 weeks pregnant when she learns her baby is not healthy. Recently amniocentesis has been performed as early as 11-1/2 weeks, allowing for vaginal abortion at 14 weeks. This means she will have felt the baby move and she will be having an abortion almost at the time when the baby could live if it were born prematurely. The abortion will be a regular labor, although the fetus is terminated first by the injection of hypo-saline solution or chemicals into the womb. Labor is induced medically, usually with prostoglandins, and may last a long time. Many women find this kind of labor a terrible experience:

"Did he advise an amniocentesis? It was borderline. He thought it would put my mind at rest. I pointed out that until I'd had this blood test my mind was at rest."

"I couldn't bear to think about it or talk about it. It was a travesty of everything I'd ever read about the glory and wonder of childbirth. It was agony, and I just wanted to be drugged until it was all over. I wouldn't let my husband be there; I couldn't have stood it for him to have to suffer it too."

Although choosing to have a termination is a terrible and shocking experience, those couples who do so find it preferable to bringing a child with severe disabilities into the world. However, some couples do choose to bring up their children with disabilities, or adopt other people's, and find great rewards in doing so:

"Of course it *was* hard at first to have a baby with Down syndrome, and we've had difficulties since he was born. But in the end we just loved him—he's our child and he's brought a lot of love into our lives."

Some mothers feel the screening tests put too much pressure

on them and medicalizes the pregnancy. "Before my first baby was born when I was 37, I had all these tests. I felt I had been taken over by doctors. I spent hours waiting at my doctor's office and at labs. They were offering a whole variety of new tests, including a blood test that was supposed to detect a person's higher risk of having a baby with Down syndrome.

"After the blood test, I got a phone call to say the result was positive. I was so distressed, I couldn't understand what they were saying at first. They explained the result was borderline but that I should come in and talk about an amniocentesis. They told me that the risk based on my age alone was 1 in 287 while with this test it was 1 in 100.

"Did he advise an amniocentesis? It was borderline. He thought it would put my mind at rest. I pointed out that until I'd had this blood test my mind *was* at rest. My husband and I talked it over, and we decided to have the amnio. I hated it, and I hated waiting for the results, which were fine. With the second baby 18 months later, I opted out. Everybody said, 'But you're at more risk,' *but I just didn't want to know.* I turned down everything, even the AFP blood test. My obstetrician was supportive; he said it was my right to have the tests or not. The pregnancy and birth were very straightforward and I had a very healthy child."

5

The Birth—Natural or Not?

In the last decade, doctors have seen considerable changes in the way childbirth is handled. More and more, mothers are able to choose their position during labor and delivery, and their wishes during the birth are given much higher profile. Hospitals may now offer birthing stools, water pools and other "natural childbirth" props. Birthing rooms in hospitals are more common. Home births may be marginally more common and accepted than they were a decade ago.

However, despite this progress, many women are still concerned that there is too much medical intervention in the process of childbirth. This is especially true for older mothers, who are considered to be at higher risk and are much more likely to receive medical intervention.

Home births are still very rare—planned home deliveries account for less than 1% of the total—and few doctors are happy about a first-time mother over 35 giving birth at home. Of course, the ultimate decision is yours, and you still have the option of a home birth if you want one, perhaps with the help of an independent midwife.

A first-time mother over 40 is likely to be offered an elective Cesarean, and this is especially true if she has had fertility problems. A high proportion of IVF babies are born by Cesarean section; first, because doctors do not want to put the baby at any risk, and second, because the whole pregnancy has become so medicalized that many mothers who could not conceive naturally doubt their ability to give birth naturally too.

This impression is backed up by a study of 195 women having

their first baby over 35, compared with another 196 women in the same situation who had a history of infertility. The study showed that the women with no history of infertility were four times more likely to have a preterm delivery (less than 37 weeks), five times more likely to undergo a Cesarean section and significantly increased rates of vaginal-assisted delivery, chronic hypertension and fibroids compared with women having their first baby between the ages of 20 and 25. Those who had suffered from infertility had twice as many elective Cesareans as those in the other group, but otherwise there was no difference in outcome.

Unfortunately, in medical litigation cases, inaction can be seen to be negligent while intervention is not. So even if in a particular labor mother and baby's chances would be best served by doing nothing, doctors may feel they have to intervene to protect themselves. When a mother is older and her baby is considered a precious baby, intervention is much more likely.

One childbirth-education teacher says that in her experience, older mothers generally feel positive about their labors. "I think they are more realistic than younger mothers."

However, mothers who opt for a natural, and in particular, a home birth, do so largely because they believe it is safer:

"I had my third child at home at the age of 35. I believe that home birth is safer if there are no special risk factors, and the labor was far quicker and in every way better than the previous two. I believe that probably more babies die as a result of infections picked up in a hospital and mismanaged, extended and messed-around-with labor in the hospital than would die at home in the rare event that something goes wrong. However, I do accept that at 35 with a first baby I would not have had the confidence to have a home birth, and if I had no children or had a history of infertility I would probably feel different too."

Marianne, pregnant with her first baby at 39 after two years of infertility treatment, disagreed. "This might be my only baby. I'll do whatever the doctors suggest. I'd like a natural birth, of course, but if things go wrong, if they suggest a Cesarean, I'll go along with it."

One childbirth-education teacher says that in her experience, older mothers generally feel positive about their labors. "I think they are more realistic than the younger mothers. They want a baby rather than a wonderful natural-childbirth experience." However, older mothers may have to stand their ground if they are under pressure to allow intervention in the childbirth process. And, like all mothers, they will have

Every labor is different for every woman.

to make a choice. This means finding out what the options are and understanding what labor, both normal and with complications, involves.

⌇ The stages of labor

Labor is divided into three clear stages. The first stage is when the muscles of the womb contract to pull open the cervix or neck of the uterus so the baby's head can come through. These contractions build in intensity. You do not push during the first stage. In the second stage, you push *with* the contractions to move the baby out of the uterus. The second stage ends with the birth of the baby. The third stage is the expulsion of the placenta (afterbirth).

Every labor is different for every woman. That's why it is so difficult for those who have never had a baby to find out what the experience is likely to be like. Labor begins in a number of different ways. Sometimes the first sign is a "show"—you will see the blood-tinged, gelatinous plug that has sealed the entrance to the uterus come out. In some women, the waters break first—this can result in a dramatic gush of fluid, or it can simply be perceived as a slow leak. If the waters leak for more than 24 hours without labor getting well under way, contact your doctor or midwife. Once the waters have broken, the baby is exposed to infection.

The most common sign labor is beginning is a cramp-like pain, similar to the onset of the menstrual period, in your lower abdomen or back. You will probably soon feel this pain turn into distinct contractions, which you can feel as a tightening and hardening of the abdomen accompanied by growing discomfort or pain. These contractions differ from the contractions felt throughout the pregnancy only in their greater intensity. As labor progresses, the contractions become stronger and closer together and also last a little longer.

The duration of the early part of labor varies greatly—some women find the contractions continue without becoming too painful for hours or even days. Others find they build up very rapidly. You are usually asked to report to the hospital when the contractions are about five minutes apart. You should know how long it takes you to get to the hospital. You do need to factor that time into your departure plan! You will not want to be traveling if the contractions are very strong and you are in great discomfort, so go when you are ready.

Many women prefer to spend the early part of labor at home in familiar surroundings, able to wander around and make a cup of decaffeinated tea and feel everything is normal. The stress of going to the hospital too soon has been known to stop a labor that has just started.

When you arrive at the hospital, you will be checked: Notes

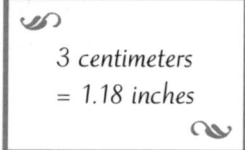

3 centimeters = 1.18 inches

will be taken, your contractions will be timed, your abdomen will be examined and someone will listen to the baby's heartbeat and then give you an internal examination to see how far your cervix has dilated. This is usually measured in centimeters; half dilation is 5cm or so and full dilation is approximately 10cm. Some nurses will talk of "two fingers" dilated—a finger is about equal to a centimeter. Often it takes a lot longer to dilate the first few centimeters than the last, because the contractions at the beginning of labor are not as strong. Some women, especially those who have had babies before, find that they are already well dilated without knowing it when they arrive at the hospital.

Many women find internal examinations during labor very uncomfortable, if not actually painful. Make sure they are done as soon as one contraction is over so you are not actually being examined during a contraction. If you find an internal examination is too uncomfortable while lying on your back, ask the doctor or midwife if he or she can examine you while you are lying on your side. Unless progress is slow, you don't necessarily have to agree to more internal examinations, although this can help check how the labor is going.

When you arrive at the hospital, your baby's heartbeat will usually be routinely monitored with an external monitor. This is tied around your tummy with a belt. You will be asked to keep still so your movements do not interfere with the reading. Most women find this very restricting. If all seems well, the monitor will be removed after 20 or 30 minutes—it may be replaced again at some point in the labor just to check that the baby is not distressed.

It is a good idea to tell the staff when you arrive if you have any strong feelings about the way you want the labor conducted. Once labor has really started, you may find yourself swept along by events. Most hospitals today are aware that women should be given a choice about pain relief and about the position they would like to adopt to deliver the baby. Also raise any queries about episiotomies, clamping and cutting the cord, anything else you wish to know and any other worries you may have. Ideally you will have discussed this with your doctor or healthcare professional beforehand. Any strong views should be recorded in your notes.

⁓ The first stage

During the first stage of labor, the cervix thins and softens and then dilates to allow the baby's head to pass through the birth canal. When the cervix is fully open it is considered "10cm dilated." This marks the transition from the first to the second stage.

Once labor has begun, contractions tend to become stronger as labor progresses, though they tend not to get closer together than about every three minutes. This means you usually get a break in between to recover from each contraction before the next one begins. Progress is not always uniform; occasionally contractions seem to run into one another, and sometimes a very strong contraction will be followed by a weaker one.

Once the woman is fully dilated, she may experience some strange symptoms. Shivering, trembling, sweating or nausea are all common. Some mothers feel restless and want to change position, often into the position in which they want to deliver the baby. At the end of each contraction the mother may begin to feel that she wants to bear down and begin to push the baby out. When the healthcare professional sees these signals, she will probably want to do an internal exam and check that you are fully dilated. If so, you are ready to begin the second stage. If you are not quite fully dilated, the nurse or midwife may ask you to "pant" during the contractions to help you resist the urge to bear down.

The second stage

Most women having an active labor find that the pushing sensation is a reflex and they can't stop themselves. Usually women know instinctively to take a deep breath, lowering the diaphragm and putting pressure on the uterus. A series of short pushes at this time can be more effective than one long push. An upright or semi-upright position is helpful in promoting the process; if you are lying down you actually have to push the baby *uphill* because of the angle of the birth canal. Most women also instinctively push with each contraction and rest in between.

With each contraction the baby should descend lower into the birth canal. At some point the baby's head will become visible from the outside (crowning); this is an exciting moment for a partner or birth companion who is present.

With each contraction the baby should descend lower into the birth canal. At some point the baby's head will become visible from the outside (crowning); this is an exciting moment for a partner or birth companion who is present. The mother can be encouraged to know that the baby is really there and about to be born. Just before the birth, the perineum begins to stretch to its widest. This can cause a stretching and stinging sensation. If you seem likely to tear, an episiotomy may be made (see page 116); otherwise the tissues become numb when stretched further. Once the baby's head has crowned, it will slip out; another contraction should deliver the shoulders and then the rest of the baby.

When the baby is born it may look strange; somewhat gray-colored and slimy with vernix and some blood. (Vernix is a waxy substance that helps protect the baby's skin from fluids in the amniotic sac.) When the baby draws breath—and usually cries loudly—the color will change to a healthier pink. If the baby is breathing normally you will be able to hold your baby, discover whether it's a boy or girl, count the fingers and toes and begin to get to know one another. Some mothers will want to put the baby straight to the breast.

⁓ The third stage

This is the delivery of the afterbirth. This stage may take up to 30 minutes. The umbilical cord, its job done, may be pulled gently, and the doctor or midwife may press her hand on your abdomen to assist delivery of the placenta. The uterus continues to contract. Your abdomen may be massaged to help the process along. If bleeding is heavy, you may receive medications in an effort to reduce the risk of postpartum hemorrhage.

Soon after the birth is a good time to put the baby to the breast for the first time, because research has shown that the sooner after the birth a baby feeds, the more likely it is that breast-feeding will be successfully established. In nature, the baby's sucking at the breast helps with delivery of the afterbirth. Not all mothers and babies are ready for a breast-feed, however, so don't feel rushed; take the time you need to get to know one another.

⌒ Risks for the older mother

Many older women fear that childbirth will be much riskier for them than for younger women, and riskier for the baby, too. This is true to a certain extent, but recent research has shown that it is not much riskier. Even where much older mothers, in their forties or fifties, are concerned, the risks may have been exaggerated. In the past, most older mothers had also had a larger number of children, the birth was more likely to have been unplanned and unwanted, and the mother may have been in poorer health. The fit woman who chooses to have a baby later may well be at lower risk than the figures would lead her to believe.

Modern hospital care and prenatal screening reduce a lot of the risks, and while the safest time to have a baby is still between 20 and 25, a mother in her late thirties who is fit and healthy, eats well and takes care of herself in pregnancy is likely to do as well or better than a younger woman who has not taken care of herself. The number of children you have had and the spacing between them is important too: The risks for the first and fourth or more births are greater than for second or third births, and the risks go up if you have a baby within two years of the previous delivery. If you have had a child before, it doesn't matter how long ago this was; a second birth is still likely to be quicker and easier.

Recent research shows that childbirth is not much riskier for older mothers and their babies than it is for younger mothers.

One reason for the greater risk of pregnancy and childbirth for the older mother is that she is more likely to suffer from diabetes, cardiovascular disease and other illnesses that affect pregnancy. If the mother does not suffer from a pre-existing disease, the risks are much lower. However, there are specific risks attached to pregnancy and these tend to increase with age. The risk of hypertension among older mothers increases by about 50%. The risk of pre-eclampsia, hemorrhage following the birth and dysfunctional labor (when the cervix does not dilate properly) are more prevalent in women over 35. The incidence of placenta previa, when the placenta covers the entrance to the uterus and can cause hemorrhage before or during the birth, or other forms of postpartum hemorrhage, increases with age and with the number of pregnancies. For first-time mothers, the risk goes up from 3% for those under 25 to 5% for those over 35. The risk doubles for mothers having a fourth child.

However, it may be true that the higher incidence of dysfunctional labor, Cesarean section and other problems could be caused by obstetric intervention in the older mother. If this baby is a more precious one because of previous infertility problems or because the mother is unlikely to conceive again, then doctors are inclined to intervene on behalf of the baby at a slightly greater risk to the mother. There is an increased risk that if the baby is overdue, the placenta of an older woman will fail sooner than that of a woman in her twenties and fail to nourish the baby properly. In that case, birth is more likely to be induced. Induction means that labor is more likely to be intensely painful, requiring pain relief and further intervention. It is also likely to be linked to dysfunctional labor, because the cervix is not yet ready to dilate. The higher rate of Cesarean-section delivery is probably linked more to caution on the part of doctors than to any substantial increase in the risk to mother or baby.

There is some controversy about whether older mothers have longer labors than younger women. Some obstetricians have said they have observed that women over 35 tend to have longer labors, perhaps because the cervix doesn't dilate as quickly in older women. It is known that Cesarean sections are more common among older mothers.

The other potential risks of birth are risks to the baby. Women over 35 have about three times the risk of miscarrying and about twice the risk of losing their baby before, during or after the birth. There is also a small increased risk in prematurity for infants of women aged 35 to 44, but this is only slightly higher than for infants of mothers in their twenties and thirties. One Swedish study showed that the risk of preterm birth for mothers aged 30 to 34 was 20% more than in mothers aged 20 to 24, from 35 to 39 was 70% more, and over 40 the rate was double. The rate of low-birth-weight babies was also about double for women over 35. Also, as we have seen, older mothers have a greater risk of having a baby with abnormalities, and this may be responsible for some neonatal deaths. A recent U.S. study of mainly first-time mothers who are professional women over 35, however, showed no evidence of older mothers being at greater risk of pre-term delivery, of having a small-for-dates baby or a baby who died in the prenatal period.

⤸ Pain relief in labor

The pain of labor is quite different from other kinds of pain. It is the pain of your body doing a hard and laborious job, not the pain of being in any way harmed. However, labor is normally painful to some degree. Many people have tried to gloss around this or give the impression that, properly prepared and armed with breathing exercises and the right attitude, you will not feel pain. This means many women are taken by surprise and believe they have failed when they *do* experience intense pain in labor and feel they need some relief from it.

We know fear and tension can create additional pain in labor and make it intolerable. If you tense all your muscles and fight the contractions, you make it much more difficult for your body to do its job. You need to think, therefore, in terms of *helping your body through the contractions.* This thinking is behind the various breathing and preparation techniques that are taught to women in prenatal classes during pregnancy. By accepting the pain and dealing with it, many women find they do not need painkilling drugs, which might also interfere with their being in control. For others experiencing a long and difficult labor, painkilling drugs may provide much-needed relief.

⌐ Breathing techniques

Slow, deep breathing will help you relax between, and at the beginning and end of, contractions. At the height of a contraction, it may help to breathe quickly and lightly, taking air into the top part of your lungs only. (Do that for just a short while.) During the transition between the first and second stages, when you may feel a desire to push out the baby, your doctor or midwife may ask you to wait till she is sure the cervix is fully dilated. At that point, short, rapid, panting breaths may help you overcome the desire to push.

⌐ Pain-relieving drugs

A number of pain-relieving drugs are available to women in labor. They are particularly useful if you are experiencing a very long labor, if the baby is presenting the wrong way (see below) or if you are becoming exhausted. These drugs, however, can pass into the baby's bloodstream and affect the baby, or may affect the progress of the labor. Many women find it useful to wait a little between the moment they first feel that they may want pain relief and deciding to accept it. In the meantime, they may find labor is progressing so well that they are nearly ready for the baby to be born. If progress is slow, however, or there is some problem, they can always decide to accept some pain relief.

⌒ *Meperidine hydrochloride*

This drug, most commonly known by its trade name Demerol®, provides pain relief. It reduces anxiety and thus pain; however, not all women find it is an effective form of pain relief. Some find it makes them feel heavy and out of control without helping the pain much. Demerol crosses the placenta and can affect the baby, making it drowsy at birth, especially if the drug is given close to delivery. (It should be given at least two hours before the baby is born; this means it cannot always be given at the point in the labor when the woman needs it most.) Some babies even need resuscitation after the birth. Many are sleepy and slow at breastfeeding. This medication can also make the mother feel sick.

⌒ *Epidural anesthesia*

An epidural consists of a local anesthetic that completely numbs the abdomen and legs, thus removing all sensation of contractions. If an epidural is timed just right, it can be allowed to wear off for the second stage so that you can feel and push with each contraction, thus helping the baby out. It seems to have little or no effect on the baby. The main potential problem is that, because some women cannot feel anything, they cannot participate in the second stage of labor, which is likely to be prolonged. The baby is more likely to be delivered with forceps. However, the correlation may be due to the fact women who are having difficult labors anyway are likely to ask for epidural anesthesia.

It seems to have little or no effect on the baby.

An epidural is injected into the epidural space in the spine, between the vertebrae and the membrane enclosing the spinal cord. You will be asked to lie on your left side and to draw up your legs to make as tight a ball as possible. This position makes it easier for the anesthetist to put the needle into the epidural space. You will be given a local anesthetic so you do not feel the tube being inserted. After that, the anesthetic is put in. It feels like a cold fluid running down your legs. The catheter is left in your back so the epidural can be "refreshed;" you will also normally have a catheter put in to empty your bladder because you will not be able to control this yourself. An intravenous drip is usually set up too, in case your blood pressure falls suddenly, which can happen with an epidural.

For some women, an epidural is the answer to a difficult labor:

"I had been in labor for hours, with strong contractions, but I wasn't dilating much. I became exhausted and thought I couldn't take any more. They offered me an epidural, and I accepted reluctantly. I have to say the effect was wonderful. Within a few minutes, I was sitting up and talking to the nurses and felt like I could cope again."

Epidurals can cause problems. About 20% of the time, the epidural does not take and provides inadequate pain relief, sometimes along one side only. Occasionally—in about one in 100 cases—the needle punctures the membrane enclosing the spinal cord. This means you are more heavily anesthetized and may suffer headaches lasting up to a week after the birth. Very rarely, in about one in 100,000 cases, permanent damage can result.

"I hated it. First the anesthetist had trouble getting it in. In fact, a little piece of plastic tubing broke off and is still floating around somewhere in my spine. Then I had all these tubes and drips set up, and I couldn't get up and walk for hours after the birth. I didn't feel or see the baby born at all because I could feel nothing. I had no idea it would be like that. And, because I couldn't push, he was delivered by forceps—so now I have all the pain of an episiotomy, which I could have done without."

Women having an epidural should be aware that they are often beginning a chain of medical intervention they might otherwise have done without. On the other hand, if the labor is likely to be difficult, it means you are spared a lot of pain and are already anesthetized if the baby has to be delivered by forceps. And if you should need an emergency Cesarean, the epidural will enable you to be awake and avoid a general anesthetic when your baby is born.

⁓ *Pudendal block*

This painkilling injection can be made into the vaginal wall with a special needle. With it, you will feel no pain at all from the delivery, and is especially useful when forceps are used. It may be used in conjunction with Demerol.

Local anesthetics are also given if an episiotomy is necessary and for any stitching done on the perineum afterward.

⟳ Difficult labors

Normally the baby is born with the head down, facing backwards, so the widest part of the baby's head passes through the widest part of the pelvis. The baby's head pressing down on the cervix helps it dilate, and the baby rotates as it is born, helping the body slip out behind the head.

Some babies, however, are born in a different position. This normally causes problems in labor. A posterior presentation means that the baby faces forward; its spine can press against the mother's as it moves down, causing her pain and slowing labor. And because the widest part of the baby's head is passing through the narrowest part of the pelvis, the baby can get stuck here more easily, again prolonging labor and sometimes requiring the use of forceps.

A breech birth occurs when the baby does not turn, so that the head is not born first; breech babies are normally born buttocks-first, occasionally feet-first. About four births in a hundred are breech. Most breech births are straightforward, though you are most likely to need intervention, especially in a first birth. Many women are advised to have an epidural; usually the baby's head is delivered with forceps to protect it, and you are likely to have an episiotomy to help the baby's head out. If you wind up needing an emergency Cesarean, the epidural will already be set up.

⌒ Medical intervention

Over the past decade or two, hospitals have increasingly used a variety of techniques that have revolutionized the process of childbirth. Most of these are intended to save lives, and frequently they do. However, many interventions have become routine in some hospitals, thus interfering with the birth process for many mothers who are not at risk. Hospitals are now more likely to discuss any possible intervention with you. You should make your views clear, although obviously everyone involved should accept that intervention may be necessary in case of an emergency.

⌒ Episiotomy

An episiotomy is a small incision made in the perineum, the skin between the vagina and the anus, to enlarge the vaginal opening and help the delivery of the baby's head. The cut is made with scissors under a local anesthetic when the baby's head comes into view. Done properly, the perineum will have stretched very thin and the cut can be made with a minimum of damage and bleeding. An episiotomy should not be necessary in a normal delivery, and you can ask not to have one if you prefer.

However, there is some controversy over whether it is better to have a small episiotomy or risk tearing the perineum when the baby's head is born. Some feel that a small tear is better and heals more rapidly, while others believe it is easier to sew up a clean cut. You should not be in great pain when the stitches are put in; if you are, ask to have more local anesthetic.

⌒ Induction

This is an artificial way of starting labor. Labor may be induced if all indications are the baby is overdue or if there is some need to deliver the baby early. Normally you will not be allowed to go much more than two weeks past your due date if the dates are firm and have been confirmed by ultrasound. There is some risk that the placenta will not be functioning as well by then. This is a particular risk in older mothers. Induction doesn't always work. Then the mother may be under pressure to have a Cesarean.

"They took me in when the baby was due and said they'd like to induce me. They said that the placenta fails quickly in older mothers and I was 47. They said there was no sign of placental failure, but that this was a fact. They tried to induce me and it failed. The next day they tried again, but the doctor said, 'Let's do a Cesarean, we want a healthy baby.' So they did."

Tests can be done to find out that the placenta is working normally. You may

Labor can be started artificially in several ways.

also be asked to keep a record of the fetus' movements. If there is evidence the baby is not growing well, that fetal movements are becoming infrequent or the mother is suffering from high blood pressure, then induction will almost certainly be recommended. By this time, many women are quite willing for the birth to be induced:

"The last few months of pregnancy I was in and out of the clinic having tests. I had an agonizing pain under the ribs, which I knew was from the baby, but they wanted to be sure it wasn't something else. I felt incredibly tired—I couldn't cope with the pain and not sleeping—so they decided to induce the birth. I was happy about that. But when I went to the hospital they told me I was too tired to cope with labor—to go home, rest for a week, not do anything. 'Then, if the baby doesn't come, we'll induce it next week.'"

Labor can be started artificially in several ways. The membranes containing the waters can be broken if the baby is overdue or near term. This usually starts labor. But if it doesn't, other intervention will be needed. That's because if the baby isn't delivered within 24 hours after the waters have been broken, he or she is at risk of infection. An artificial rupture of the membranes (ARM) or amniotomy is performed with an instrument that looks like a long crochet hook. This procedure is normally painless. The technique is also used to speed up labor. Once the waters have broken, the baby's head, unprotected by the bag of waters, presses harder against the cervix, encouraging the uterus to contract. The contractions will become much stronger and you will also feel some of the waters gushing out with each contraction.

Prostaglandin suppositories may be used to start labor. These are usually inserted into the vagina. The effect of the hormones close to the cervix is to trigger labor. A man's sperm contains prostaglandin, which is why women at risk of a premature birth should avoid full sexual intercourse and why one of the best natural ways to induce labor is to make love. A prostaglandin-induced labor works well because, once started, it can proceed without further intervention.

If labor does not start in any other way, an oxytocin drip is used. Oxytocin is the hormone that naturally causes the contractions of labor. Various artificial forms of oxytocin can be used. (The trade name is Pitocin®.) A drip is inserted into your arm—you can ask to have it put into the arm you use least. You can also ask to have a long tube connecting you to the drip so you can move around and change position as much as possible. Contractions caused when you are on an oxytocin drip are usually stronger, longer and more painful. You may also find that you are plunged into the height of labor without having time to adjust to gradually increasing contractions. This can make the pain more difficult to cope with. In fact, pain relief is often necessary in these circumstances. This in itself can lead to further intervention.

⌒ Electronic fetal monitoring

Once labor is established, the baby's heartbeat and the strength of your contractions can be measured electronically. It can be reassuring to be able to hear and actually see throughout the delivery that the baby is well and not in distress, though this can also be checked using an old-fashioned ear trumpet or a fetal stethoscope. The disadvantage of electronic fetal monitoring is, you will be attached to a machine during labor. You may feel it is getting more attention than you are! You will not be free to move around. Sometimes the machines do not work well. Some women have noticed that the slightest change in the baby's heartbeat will lead to intervention, which may not have been necessary.

There is now evidence that continuous electronic fetal monitoring does not make any difference to the labor outcome as far as the baby's health and safety are concerned, although it results in a higher risk of intervention. However, in any individual case in which monitoring was not performed and a baby dies, the doctor or staff may be sued. For that reason, monitoring is almost always done to protect them, even though there may be no evidence that it is necessary.

Monitoring can be done with an external monitor strapped to your abdomen. Most women find this is awkward because they have to remain still. Also, the monitor has a tendency to slip off during a contraction:

"They kept fussing around, trying to put it back on . . . I couldn't concentrate on what I was doing. Most of the time it wasn't in the right place and we just heard a lot of noise, not the baby's heartbeat."

An internal monitor works better and is less restrictive for the mother. However, the waters must be broken and the cervix must be at least 2cm to 3cm dilated for this to be attached to the baby's head. A tiny scar, like a pinprick, will be left after the monitor is removed but it is unlikely to cause the baby much discomfort. In cases where it is thought the baby may be distressed, a blood sample may be taken from the baby's head and analyzed.

⌒ Forceps

Forceps deliveries are carried out after the first stage, when the cervix is fully dilated. Forceps are used if for some reason the baby's head is not coming down the birth canal, or if the baby is in distress and needs to be born rapidly. Premature babies may be delivered by forceps to spare their heads from being too compressed as they come through the birth canal. Forceps are also usually used to protect the baby's head in a breech birth.

If your baby needs a forceps delivery, you will be asked to lie on your back and your legs will be put into stirrups. You will receive a local anesthetic. An episiotomy will be done to increase the vaginal opening. Forceps will be gently inserted around the baby's head. Gentle pulling helps the head out. Once the head is born, the rest of the delivery occurs normally. If the baby's head faces the wrong way, forceps may be used to rotate the baby's head to help delivery.

Forceps deliveries are very safe and there is little chance of the baby being harmed in any way, although most will have marks on the head from the forceps for a few days after the birth. Forceps deliveries occur more often after a protracted labor where the mother becomes exhausted, where she has had an epidural and cannot feel to push with each contraction or where the baby's head is large or in the wrong position.

Sometimes a vacuum extractor, also called a *ventouse,* is used instead of forceps. This is a cup placed on the baby's head that is operated by a vacuum pump. It can be inserted before the cervix is fully dilated and is used, in conjunction with the mother's pushing, to deliver the baby. A small circular mark where the cup was placed shows on the baby's head for a few days after the delivery.

⌒ Cesarean section

Cesarean sections are being carried out more frequently than ever before. According to a report by the International Childbirth Educators Association's Cesarean-Options Committee (1997), "In the past 20 years, Cesarean-section rates have quintupled in the United States, to 23.8% [of all births] in 1989, and nearly quadrupled in Canada, to 18.3% in 1987-8." The rate is one in three for high-risk pregnancies (women giving birth after age 35 are currently considered to be subject to high-risk pregnancy). The main reason for this change is that the operation has become much safer than it used to be. Improvements in anesthetics have lowered the risk, especially since a planned Cesarean can now be done with an epidural rather than general anesthetic.

The development of the low, transverse "bikini cut" incision also made the operation safer and more acceptable, and decreased the risk for women who may want to have a later birth the normal way. The number of Cesareans have increased in recent years for reasons that include:

◆ Doctors are better able these days to detect babies in distress who need to be delivered this way.

◆ It reduces the use of forceps, which can carry its own risks.

◆ It is considered a safe surgery.

◆ Having had a Cesarean can predispose a woman for another in a subsequent pregnancy.

The most common reason cited for a Cesarean is that the baby's head is too big to pass through the pelvis, but other reasons include:

◆ The mother suffers from a disease, such as diabetes or chronic high blood pressure.

◆ The uterus does not contract properly, even with stimulation.

◆ There are signs of fetal distress.

◆ The placenta is wrongly positioned (placenta previa).

The mother's age is also taken into account, because it is anticipated that older mothers will have more difficult labors, and the baby may be more "precious," especially if the woman has suffered infertility or miscarriages or may not conceive again. In these circumstances a doctor may prefer to do a Cesarean than take any risk for the baby's well-being:

"The attending staff never mentioned my age at all. They didn't make me feel old. It was only at the end, when they discovered she was breech, that it suddenly came up, because they wanted me to have a Cesarean. They said, 'Well, it's your first baby, it's breech, you've had infertility problems and you're 40. This might be your only baby, so you want to be sure that nothing goes wrong.'"

⌐ What happens during a Cesarean

If you know in advance you are going to have a Cesarean, you can plan for it. You can choose to have the operation done under an epidural anesthetic. That way, you can see and participate in the birth and see or hold your baby as soon as he or she is born. Your husband or partner is also likely to be present for the entire operation. You can make plans for the extra support you will need when you come out of the hospital. If the operation is done as an emergency, however, you are likely to be given a general anesthetic, because setting up an epidural takes time. Your partner may not be able to be with you. In addition, you are likely to suffer aftereffects of the anesthetic, making it more difficult to bond with your new baby right after birth.

A typical Cesarean section usually takes about 45 minutes from start to finish. The baby is delivered in the first 5 to 10 minutes, and the rest of the operation is concerned with stitching you up. The surgeon makes a cut about 12cm long, usually horizontally and just below the "bikini line." He or she then cuts horizontally through the lower part of the uterus, where there are no main blood vessels. The bag of waters may break of its own accord or have to be broken, and the fluid is sucked away. The surgeon then puts his or her hands into the uterus and rotates the baby's head so that it appears in the incision. The surgeon helps deliver the baby's head using his or her hands, or sometimes forceps, and an assistant usually presses gently on the top part of the uterus. A drug to make the uterus contract and stop any bleeding is given, and the rest of the baby is brought out. Then the placenta is delivered. Next, the uterus is sewn up and then the abdominal wall.

Although the Cesarean section is a very safe operation, it is major surgery. The risk of complications, although small in this case, exists wherever surgery is concerned.

Although the Cesarean section is a very safe operation, it is major surgery. The risk of complications, although small in this case, exists wherever surgery is concerned. Many women experience a lot of postoperative pain and may find they cannot get comfortable for breast-feeding. Mothers often find it takes them longer to bond with their baby because they feel so uncomfortable in the days following the delivery:

"Having a Cesarean leaves you so incapacitated that it takes much longer to do things for the baby. Everything the baby does makes you feel so uncomfortable—lifting, feeding—and you are tied down with drips and bottles draining the wound for two days. Your mind is geared to you and not to the baby—it is harder to bond. Because of this I really appreciated the time I had with her at the beginning. My Cesarean was planned, so it was done with an epidural and I was awake. She was born onto me, although I couldn't feel it. I was able to hold her right away. I was able to think, 'This is *my* baby, all right,' and the three of us had about 1-1/2 hours together after the birth. Without that I think it would have been really hard."

◁ Premature delivery

No one knows what causes premature labor, nor can much be done to prevent it. Drugs can be given to try to stop labor, but the success rate is not very high and these drugs may affect the baby. Multiple pregnancies are more likely to result in the birth of premature and low-birth-weight babies, especially if the mother is having more than twins.

Prematurity is defined as much in terms of weight as it is for actual age from conception. A distinction is made between babies who are of low birth weight but born at the right time—they are known as "small-for-dates"—and babies who are born too early. About 6% or 7% of babies are born weighing less than 2,500 grams (5-1/2 pounds) and these are responsible for a large proportion of infant deaths. All low-birth-weight babies are likely to have problems adjusting to life outside the womb and to need special care.

Enormous advances have been made in the care of premature and low-birth-weight babies. Today they stand a much better chance of survival.

Babies are born "small-for-dates" for a number of reasons. Sometimes the baby does not grow enough in the last months in the womb because the mother is malnourished, smokes or drinks, suffers from pre-eclampsia or because the placenta is not working properly (placental insufficiency). Twins often do not grow as large as a single baby would, and some babies are small for genetic reasons or because they have some abnormality. If the baby appears not to be growing well in the last month or so of pregnancy and the woman suffers from pre-eclampsia or placental insufficiency, the baby may be induced. In these cases, the baby stands a better chance of survival once it has been born.

No one really knows what triggers a premature birth, because the reasons why labor starts normally are obscure. Occasionally vaginal infections may be involved. Researchers are looking into the reasons for premature delivery. They are also looking for an effective way to delay labor, if this will increase the baby's chances of survival. Drugs can be given to try to prevent premature labor, but these are not always effective. They may have unpleasant side effects, too.

However, enormous advances have been made in the care of premature and low-birth-weight babies. Today they stand a much better chance of survival. In 1982, 40% of babies weighing 1,000 grams (2 pounds) or less survived, 83% of babies weighing between 1,000 and 1,500 grams (2 to 3 pounds) survived, and 95% of babies weighing 1,500 to 2,000 grams (3 to 4-1/2 pounds) survived.

If your baby is born prematurely, but after the 28th week of pregnancy, he or she stands a good chance of survival.

Measured by gestational age, 70% of babies born at 27 or 28 weeks survive, 80% born at 29 weeks survive and at over 30 weeks the vast majority will survive. All these figures, of course, apply to babies who are given special care immediately after birth. Tiny babies of as little as 20 weeks have been known to survive, but it is rare.

It is comforting to know that if your baby is born prematurely, but after the 28th week of pregnancy, he or she stands a good chance of survival. However, going into premature labor is an alarming and frightening experience. Most mothers are completely unprepared and fear that their baby will not survive. This may color the whole birth process. The experience can be made worse by being in the wrong place:

"Ruben was born at 28-1/2 weeks. We had been on vacation when my waters started to leak, so I went to the nearest urgent-care clinic, where they really didn't have a clue about anything. We decided we had to get back to Seattle, where my doctor was. I had terrible anxiety wondering if labor really was starting and whether the baby could survive. In Seattle, we were told they couldn't stop labor because once the waters have gone, the baby is susceptible to infection. It was my second birth and a normal labor. I was advised not to have any pain relief because it would affect my baby and worsen his survival chances.

"He spent weeks in neonatal intensive care. I was terrified the whole time he wouldn't make it. In fact, one of the other babies in the neonatal intensive care unit, who was born at the same time as Ruben, died while we were there. It was just terrible. I kept thinking, 'That could be me, that could be me.'"

Premature babies are not ready to live in the environment outside the uterus. The layer of fat under the skin has not been laid down, so the premature baby cannot control his body temperature. Many preterm babies suffer from respiratory-distress syndrome. Their lungs do not contain enough of a substance called *surfactant*, which is necessary for getting enough oxygen. The baby has to make an enormous effort to breathe and without help rapidly becomes exhausted. Such babies will need to be given oxygen through a tiny tube down the nostrils or through a face mask, or with the help of a mechanical ventilator, which does the work of breathing for the baby. A ventilator is used if the baby is in real difficulty.

Some low-birth-weight babies have low blood sugar. This can also happen if the mother has diabetes or if the delivery was difficult. An intravenous drip may be set up to give the baby enough nourishment.

An incubator regulates the baby's temperature and enables the medical staff to give any necessary treatment.

Many premature babies suffer from jaundice. About half of all babies develop mild jaundice, in fact, because a newborn baby has a surplus of red blood cells. These are only broken down after birth, producing a substance called *bilirubin*. The baby's liver sometimes is immature and cannot cope with the bilirubin rapidly enough. This gives the baby's skin a yellowish tinge and we say the baby is *jaundiced*. If a baby is very jaundiced, photo therapy can be used to help the body process all the bilirubin. The baby's eyes are covered and light is shone on the baby's body. The light breaks down the pigments in the body.

That done, the baby can excrete them in its urine, and the jaundice goes away.

Almost all premature and low-birth-weight babies need to be kept in an incubator. An incubator regulates the baby's temperature and enables the medical staff to give any necessary treatment. However, it can be hard for the mother to relate to her baby if he or she is in an incubator, especially if the baby is surrounded by special tubes and equipment. Feeding can also be a problem.

All premature babies should be given breast milk if at all possible, because it contains antibodies and other factors that will help the baby fight infection. But the baby may be unable to suck. Some babies who are too weak to breast-feed may be able to suck from a bottle filled with expressed breast milk, or from a cup. Others may need to be fed through a tube. However, breast milk is the best choice for the baby, because it contains unique substances that promote the baby's growth and development. So the mother of a premature baby will usually be shown how to express breast milk to nourish the baby and to establish her milk supply for when the baby is well:

The mother of a premature baby will usually be shown how to express breast milk to nourish the baby and to establish her milk supply for when the baby is well.

"It was a huge production, going to the hospital all the time and expressing milk. For me, it was too difficult to express much at home, although I did it as much as I could. But the nurses at the hospital were wonderfully supportive. They made me feel I was really helping, was really giving my baby something no one else could. Still, it's hard. Although he's home now, he's been too weak to feed from the breast and is used to the bottle. I don't feel I can go on expressing forever, and at this point I don't think I'll establish actual breast-feeding. I plan to give it a try, though."

Some mothers cannot cope with it:

"I couldn't express my milk because all the time he was so ill, I thought he was going to die. It made me so unhappy to express milk I thought he'd never take that I couldn't go on with it."

Very small babies may look like tiny, fragile, even ugly little creatures to begin with. This may make relating to them more difficult. The cry of a premature baby may sound more like the bleat of a lamb or mew of a kitten than a baby. Many babies are so thin they look more like fledgling birds:

"She was so tiny I couldn't believe it—she weighed only 2-1/2 pounds. She hardly looked human at all, more like a little bird that had been pushed out of the nest. Because she had breathing difficulties, her little chest heaved and she made funny wheezing noises. She was surrounded by tubes and I wasn't allowed to hold her, so I felt completely unable to relate to her."

But despite their initial problems, the great majority of premature babies will thrive and eventually make up for lost time. It is important for the parents to remember, though, that their baby is really the age from the time he should have been born, not his actual birthday. One mother explains:

"Since he was born three months early, it was very difficult to explain [his size] to people. At six months from his birthday, he was of course at the stage of a normal 3-month-old baby. If I said to people, he's six months old, they would tut-tut and obviously think he was backward. So in the end I gave his age from the due date, not his birthday, to people I met casually. It was very odd to celebrate his first birthday when he was just like a nine-month-old."

By the second or third birthday, the difference between the baby's age and the developmental stage has narrowed and become unimportant—the baby has "caught up."

⌐ Stillbirth

The death of a baby is a traumatic experience and one that hospital staff may find it difficult to deal with. They are geared up to deal with the joy of birth and not the tragedy of death. At the same time, doctors and nurses may be consumed with the aftermath of the delivery or in trying to save a baby's life. They have little time for the mother and father, leaving both in a state of uncertainty:

"The delivery was awful and he was rushed off to the NICU [neonatal intensive care unit] the moment he was born. I remember they were all fussing around, giving me stitches and cleaning me up, but *nobody* mentioned the baby. I just assumed he was dead; at first I couldn't believe it. I felt numb, then I started crying. Nobody said anything to me and my husband went off to find someone who would tell him what was going on. Then they came to take me back to my room and I said, in tears, 'I'm not going, I'm not going to the ward to see those mothers and babies.' 'Why not?' they asked. 'Because my baby's dead!' I bawled. At that there was a flurry, and someone came to say he wasn't dead at all! He was in intensive care but they were sure he'd be all right, and I could go back and look at him later. It was, in fact, touch and go, but they didn't say so at the time."

If a woman is kept uninformed and uninvolved, the consequences can be quite tragic:

"It was obvious that something was wrong as soon as he was born. He was taken to the NICU immediately. There was some confusion over what different doctors said about whether he would live or not and that was hard, because I didn't know whether there was hope. Meanwhile I was in the regular maternity ward with mothers and babies. I wasn't with him when they disconnected the life-support system and let him die—there was no point in doing anything. If I had been more involved and helped by them, I think I would have chosen to be with him and to have held him when he died."

There are probably many women who would have very similar feelings and reactions. Until very recently parents were not encouraged even to see their baby, who was whisked away as soon as it was confirmed that the baby was dead. Today, hospital staffs are increasingly aware that many parents want to see their baby, accept its death and have time to grieve. This applies even if the baby is born with a congenital abnormality. The imaginings of someone who has given birth to a baby with physical abnormalities are likely to be much worse than the reality; again, seeing, being with and holding the child can help parents accept the situation:

"They said the baby was deformed and [so] I didn't want to see her. But my husband did, and he said, really it's all right, she's quite beautiful, you can look. They had wrapped her up so that her face and arms and tiny feet showed. She was very beautiful, and her face had a peaceful expression that made me immediately feel much better about her death."

A mother whose baby has died can ask not to go to the postnatal ward, but to be given a room of her own or perhaps go to the general gynecological ward. Hormones can be given to suppress the milk supply, though this is less typical now because the drugs can have side effects. The mother may continue to produce milk for some days, to her great distress. The mother whose baby has died will have all the usual hormonal and emotional changes following a birth, but no baby; she is in a kind of emotional limbo, neither a mother nor *not* a mother.

Today, hospital staffs are increasingly aware that many parents want to see their baby, accept its death and have time to grieve.

If the baby has died because of some lack of intervention or action by medical staff, parents usually take out their anger on the hospital. This can make the situation worse immediately after the baby has died: "They should have figured out he was in distress. I can't forgive them." Anger is a normal part of the grieving process; being able to blame someone can help the situation seem more bearable for the parents in the short term. Most stillbirth or neonatal deaths, however, could not have been prevented, and blaming the hospital will not bring back a baby who has died.

How the hospital staff deals with a tragedy can make an enormous difference to the experience. If you have worries, it can help to talk to your team in advance about what you would like to happen in the event of the baby's death, even if this sounds as if you are being unnecessarily morbid:

"I told them that if the baby was dead I didn't want them to whisk her away. I would like to see and hold the baby right then and deal with my emotions then and there. They brushed this aside and said of course nothing will go wrong. In fact, my baby was born perfectly healthy. But I felt it was important for me to say what I wanted in case the unthinkable happened, so we knew where we stood and I wouldn't be faced with half-truths or well-meaning attempts to protect me from reality."

Women—and men—who have experienced a baby's death are often told by doctors, hospital staff, relatives and friends to "forget about this experience—you'll have another baby soon." This is very distressing for the parents, who need to acknowledge the death and mourn the loss of their baby before going on to another pregnancy. Some hospitals will help the parents by encouraging them to see and hold the baby, perhaps taking a photograph they can keep, and discussing what sort of funeral arrangements should be made. Hospitals usually arrange for a cremation or burial free of charge, but some parents find they hastily go along with such arrangements and later are distressed because they did not attend a ceremony and because the baby is buried with others or in an unmarked grave.

Some hospitals will help the parents by encouraging them to see and hold the baby, perhaps taking a photograph they can keep.

You will also need to register the baby's birth or death. You can ask that the baby's name be recorded so that he or she can be acknowledged as your child, a real individual, and not just "a baby." If you feel the hospital is not paying attention to your wishes, be firm and ask for what you want. Taking action in this positive way may help you feel a lot better about the experience when you look back on it and help you in the natural process of grieving. (See Further Reading, starting on page 165, for helpful books.)

⌒ Bonding with your baby

Much emphasis has been placed on the importance of mothers bonding with their new baby. Sometimes bonding is described as if it were a mystical process. Often it sounds as though bonding has to take place in the early moments after the birth (or at least within the first few days) or the mother-and-child relationship will be in trouble. The process of bonding with a child is a very important one, but *everyone is different.* Some people will fall in love with their future husbands at first sight, others build a relationship slowly over the years. In the end the quality of love achieved may not have much to do with the feelings you felt at first; it is the same with a baby.

There is no doubt, though, that the nature of the delivery and the conditions at the time of the birth can help the mother relate to her baby—or hinder her. Hospitals have on the whole changed enormously in this respect:

"My first baby, whom I had in my twenties, was born the way it was for my mother: My husband wasn't there; I did what I was told. The doctor delivered the baby and I just happened to be there. The baby was taken away and bathed as soon as she was born and I was given this clean white bundle to look at. We only saw the babies at feeding time, every four hours, and I had to struggle to breast-feed. My husband only saw his child hours later, at visiting time.

"With this baby it was completely different. Not only was Bill there the birth, he'd come along for tests and things throughout the pregnancy. It was a pleasant room with pretty wallpaper and curtains, and we could bring our own things with us, like a CD-player with our favorite music. The birth was fine, although I had a massive hemorrhage afterwards and the baby needed resuscitation. But as soon as all that had been taken care of, they left us, melted away, turned down the lights, and we were left on our own with the soft lighting, pretty wallpaper and music."

Nowadays most mothers who breast-feed their baby will be allowed or encouraged to put the baby to the breast soon after the birth. The baby may be delivered straight onto the mother's tummy. In any case, both parents are likely to be able to see and hold him immediately, before he is washed and weighed. Despite this kind of care, however, not all mothers feel a rush of love:

"It was a perfect birth. I saw him born. They delivered him onto my tummy, and there he was, a perfect, beautiful baby with wide-open eyes; he didn't yell—he looked all around him. I didn't feel a thing. In fact, at this, the greatest moment of my life, all I said was, "Is that my baby?" I was completely exhausted and drained of any emotion. My husband held him while I was stitched up—I'm sure he bonded with him, because I could hear this long conversation going on, my husband talking to him and our baby gazing up at his face. Then they put him to the breast, but again I didn't feel anything. It was a strange blur.

"Afterwards, when I was back in the room I shared with two

other new mothers, I would look at this tiny baby next to me and think, this is it, you should be overjoyed, this is your perfect baby. To tell the truth, I don't think I really loved him then. I mothered him and did everything I should, felt protective and concerned, but only now that he's a person, walking and starting to talk, can I say I really love him."

Still, the importance of that early time after the birth cannot be overestimated. It can be important to have a time of peace and quiet together before being plunged into all the problems and worries of parenting. The time immediately after the birth provides a perfect time for this. To begin with, the baby is usually awake and alert and not yet frantic to feed. The parents can hold and talk to him and feel that he is really theirs. There don't have to be any other distractions at this time. Tasks such as bathing the baby and tidying up the mother can wait. The short time right after the birth is a unique moment that should be fully exploited.

The time immediately after the birth provides a perfect time for bonding. The baby is usually wide awake and alert and not yet frantic to feed.

Some studies show that mothers who have been separated from their babies immediately after the birth find it harder to bond, and this does seem to be true of women who have had Cesarean sections or whose babies have had special care. But other factors are at work as well. Women who have had infertility problems or have suffered the loss of a baby may have held back their emotions in case they do not get their longed-for baby. It can be difficult to release these emotions when the baby becomes a reality:

"I had taken a long time to conceive and also had a miscarriage. I started to think I would never have a baby. When he was born, I couldn't just switch on the love I'd bottled up all those years. I had to take time to get used to the fact this was real—and to get to know him."

Some women find that being in the hospital makes it more difficult for them to relate to their babies. With all the activity going on, the streams of visitors to you and other mothers, the comings and goings of doctors and nurses, there can seem to be little time alone to get to know your baby. Worse, your partner can only visit. When he *is* with you, there is little privacy:

"The next day I had the blues that everyone seems to have, when your milk comes in and your hormones are all upside-down. I didn't feel like I could cope, so I hid in a room off the nursery to cry. Then another mother came to find me and said, 'Your baby's screaming its head off, what are you doing?' So I went back to feed the baby. She came with me, and I know she was trying to help. She said, 'We've all had crying jags, don't worry about it.' But she kept making comments about how I was feeding the baby. I just wanted to be alone, and I wanted my husband there, especially at night. Right after the baby was born, I lay awake at night wanting just to cuddle him. And when he did come of course all I could get was a peck on the cheek with everyone else around."

Many women feel that the time after the birth should be for them and their families alone:

"After my Cesarean, I left after a 3-day stay in the hospital. They didn't want me to go so soon, but I wanted the three of us to be together. I thought we'd blunder along together better than here, where all this 'help' is clinical and not emotional."

"I came home after one day because I didn't want my little boy to see us in the hospital. I didn't want him to find me stuck in a strange hospital bed and the baby in a plastic crib and unable to be ourselves. I thought he should see us all at home and get to know the baby there, to have his mother with him and not to have to go away and leave us in a strange place."

Today it is accepted for the father to be present at the birth of the child. This is one of the greatest changes that has taken place in the last few decades of childbearing practice. (Of course, before hospital births became the norm, many fathers would have been present at home for their child's birth.) Few hospitals have any objection to the father's presence, even at difficult births like forceps deliveries or Cesareans. The father is often involved in holding the baby after the birth while the mother is stitched or cleaned up and while the afterbirth is delivered. Visiting hours have also been made more flexible so that at most hospitals fathers have unlimited visiting and can get to know their child a little before the family is at home together.

Many fathers find the whole experience of birth exciting and rewarding. These fathers say they feel closer to their children because of it. Others may also feel that they were helpless and couldn't do anything to prevent their partner's suffering, which they found upsetting. Not all men provide the expected help:

"He turned green and looked terrible. I felt sorry for him. But his reaction made it worse for me in a way. I kept thinking I *can't* yell, it'll upset him too much."

"At the worst stage in the labor I asked him how he was feeling, and he said, 'I'd rather be home in bed.' I think he just felt helpless. It was like he betrayed me, he was so insensitive at that moment—but then, it's very hard for him to show his feelings, and he had to put on a masculine front."

"They offered me pain relief and I decided to take it, despite our plans for a natural birth. But he refused to let me take anything! He kept telling the staff, 'She doesn't mean it, she's OK.' In retrospect I'm pleased, in a way. But at the time I thought, 'What does HE know about how I'm feeling?!'"

At most hospitals, fathers have unlimited visiting and can get to know their child a little before the family is at home together.

Other women say they could not have managed without their partners:

"He was wonderful. It helped, knowing he was there. He really soothed me. When the baby was born he was so thrilled, he was beside himself. He was holding the baby as soon as they would give him to him—I wouldn't have had him miss that for the world."

When the father is unable or unwilling to attend, most hospitals will allow you to have a close friend or relative as your birth partner to provide support and help. Sometimes the hospital staff seems to discourage an early discharge because they feel you will be unsupported at home. This is often not the case. Many women find that they can relax and solve problems once they have sole charge of the baby and do not feel they have to get permission all the time to do what they feel most comfortable doing.

However, there has been a steady trend towards women going home from hospitals earlier. The once-accepted week-long stay has gone down to an average of 2 or 3 days, and the majority of women with no problems are now discharged after 24 to 48 hours.

➭ Breast-feeding

The majority of new mothers leaving the hospital today breast-feed their babies, at least at the beginning—about 60%. This is especially true for middle-class and professional

When the father is unable to attend, most hospitals will allow you to have a close friend or relative as your birth partner to provide support and help.

women, which the majority of older mothers are likely to be. Age does not seem to have any great effect on breast-feeding. It is not commonly known that any woman who has had a baby can breast-feed, and that in other cultures grandmothers breast-feed their daughter's children. Occasionally a much older mother may find it a problem to produce enough milk, due to hormonal problems, but this is rare.

Many hospitals now give great support and encouragement to mothers who want to breast-feed, recognizing that it is the best food for a baby and that there are emotional rewards for the nursing mother. The American Academy of Pediatrics issued a strongly worded policy in 1997 that suggests women nurse for six to 12 months, because of a strong association between breast-feeding and immunities for babies from a variety of ailments. But some women decide they do not want to breast-feed. There is no reason to feel guilty about this. There are excellent baby formulas available now that are made to match the nutrition of mother's milk as closely as possible. Bottle-fed babies also thrive. Love is more important than the way you choose to feed, though many mothers choose to express their love through breast-feeding.

Breast-feeding is best for a baby because it is a living substance transmitted directly from mother to baby, containing white blood cells, antibodies and other substances that help protect the baby against disease. We haven't yet identified all these protective properties. It is composed of exactly the right nutrients for human babies and is produced in exactly the quantities the baby demands.

After the birth a mother produces colostrum, a yellowish fluid rich in antibodies, which protects the baby from infection. Colostrum also contains protein, water and minerals in just the right proportion for the baby's first few days, and a natural laxative, which helps the baby's bowels start working. When the milk comes in, it is also perfectly balanced for the baby's needs. The milk changes slightly in composition as the baby grows. Research has shown that milk produced by the mothers of premature babies is different from normal breast milk, and is ideally suited for them.

When the baby first goes to the breast and sucks, it takes the watery foremilk stored in ducts behind the areola, the pigmented area around the nipple. The baby's sucking sends a message to the brain to let down the bulk of the milk, and the hormone oxytocin— the same hormone that makes the womb contract in labor and at orgasm—is released, causing the muscles around the glands producing the milk to contract and squeeze the milk through the breast to the nipple. The baby usually takes the bulk of the feeding in the first ten minutes or so at the breast. But enough milk is always produced so the feeding can last much longer than this.

Breast milk is composed of exactly the right nutrients for human babies and is produced in exactly the quantities the baby demands.

Most hospitals have made-up bottles of formula readily available. This is a great temptation to a mother who is having problems with breast-feeding and who is very tired. If you are certain you want to breast-feed, resist this temptation! It takes some time to establish breast-feeding and there are often some initial problems, but they should resolve themselves shortly. Some babies who get used to the bottle find it is more difficult to take the breast. Babies who have had bottles sometimes reject the breast altogether. Mothers who want to avoid cow's milk because of eczema and asthma in the family should also resist the temptation to give a bottle.

⌒ Starting feeding

It is important to feel comfortable and relaxed when you are breast-feeding. Get into a position that puts no strain on your back, shoulders or limbs. Hold the baby comfortably, perhaps resting on a pillow so he is at the right height. Use his "rooting" reflex to get him to feed—brush the cheek nearest the breast and he will turn his head, mouth open, to latch on.

Milk produced by the mothers of premature babies is different from normal breast milk, and is ideally suited for them.

It is very important to see that the baby has a large part of the areola, the area around the nipple, in the lower part of his mouth. (If he takes just the nipple into his mouth you will soon become sore, and he will not be able to get out the milk.) Once he is latched on and feeding correctly, you shouldn't feel any great discomfort, even if your nipples are sore. If you do feel pain, remove his mouth by slipping your little finger in the corner of his mouth to break the suction, and try again.

At the end of the feed the baby is likely to be sucking very gently, for comfort only. If this is sending him to sleep there is probably little point in removing him until he is satisfied. If your nipples are sore or if you are tired or need to do something else, don't feel guilty about removing him.

Breast-feeding does not come naturally to the majority of women. It is easy to be put off by initial difficulties. Many mothers need a great deal of support to establish breast-feeding, particularly after a Cesarean:

"The most difficult time was the first few weeks. Because I couldn't exclusively feed him I had to supplement, which was disappointing. I did everything to try and get him to breast-feed exclusively. I had a lot of support. But because of the Cesarean, I had an infection and had to take antibiotics, which were not compatible with breast-feeding. I didn't question it at the time, although I now I wish I had. All this acted against my breast-feeding the baby. And, of course, they put him on formula right

Breast-feeding: Problems and Solutions

❖ **Sore nipples**

At first, the nipples may become sore and painful. You may get small blisters. Sore, puffy, red nipples may be caused by thrush, which can also affect the baby.

Check to make sure the baby has its mouth open wide enough and is not tugging on the nipple. Sunlight and fresh air help sore nipples heal. Rub a little expressed breast milk on them, too. Medicated cream can be prescribed for thrush.

❖ **Cracked nipples**

If the baby is latched on incorrectly, the nipple may crack. The nipple is very painful and may bleed.

If you latch on the baby correctly, you can still feed from a cracked nipple. You may need to express milk from that breast for 24 hours to allow the crack to heal.

❖ **Engorged breasts**

This often happens when the milk first comes in, before the baby gets feeding established. If the breasts are too full, the areola can become too hard for the baby to latch on properly. A vicious cycle starts.

Express a little milk before a feed to soften the breast and help the baby latch on properly. Warm washcloths or a warm bath will relieve the breasts. Or, try putting cabbage leaves inside your nursing bra.

away in the hospital—which I would also question if I did it again. We got through it, but it was hard. I think because I was older I should have known how to cope, that somehow I shouldn't have felt so demoralized in those first few weeks."

With other difficulties to overcome, the initial experience may be unrewarding as well as discouraging. It may take time and a lot of encouragement to get over these hurdles:

Breast-feeding: Problems and Solutions, con't.

❧ **Blocked duct**

You may notice a hard lump in one breast; the tissue above it may seem engorged. If the blockage doesn't clear, the spot may become red and infected. Mastitis can result, in which the breast becomes red and you run a high temperature. It is important to continue feeding the baby. If you stop, the mastitis will worsen.

Put the baby to the blocked breast first. Try to position him so his lower jaw is where the blocked duct is. Massage the breast towards the nipple and use warm washcloths over that area before a feed. If mastitis results, continue feeding, and see a doctor. He or she may prescribe antibiotics.

❧ **Breast abscess**

If mastitis does not clear up, you may get a breast abscess. If you have continued to breast-feed despite mastitis, this development is rare.

See a doctor to have the abscess taken care of through aspiration or surgery. You can usually continue to feed the baby. In any case, you can continue to breast-feed from the unaffected breast.

"After my Cesarean it was hard for me to establish breast-feeding. Now that my daughter is six weeks old, we have finally figured it out. They said it takes longer for the milk to come in and it's difficult to hold a baby when you're feeling so sore after a C-section. Also my breasts were so painful! The nipples were so sore—nobody had prepared me for that. I kept thinking, 'Where is this wonderful experience? Am I normal?' Finally, talking to a relative helped. She said, 'Yes, it *is* painful but it will get better.' I think in a way I had too much information and advice—I changed to the bottle because the hospital nurse advised me to, and then went back to the breast. All I needed was for someone to say, 'Yes, it's awful at the beginning. I've been through it, and it does become rewarding eventually.'"

"No one told me you could breast- AND bottle-feed."

Many women are given the impression that they must either totally breast-feed or bottle-feed and there is no "in between." It may be true that it is important to breast-feed entirely for the early weeks while you are building up a good supply, but the occasional "relief bottle" a partner or caregiver provides can be timely and prevent a mother from giving up entirely:

"I only breast-fed for six weeks. It was too demanding—she never lasted for two hours and wanted to be fed all the time. No one told me you could breast- *and* bottle-feed. So I stopped and put her on a bottle, which she took just fine. I didn't ask advice from my doctor's office nurse—we didn't get along. I'd feel fine until I saw her and then she'd upset me. That didn't help. At the well-baby clinic I knew I'd have to wait so long that I didn't bother."

Even if you are going back to work soon after the birth, breast-feeding for the first few weeks gives the baby the best possible start and you can continue to breast-feed morning and night if you choose.

Breast-feeding is a completely different experience compared to bottle-feeding. It doesn't follow a strict schedule or routine, which was prevalent a generation ago. Breast-feeding mothers, who know they should feed on demand and as often as every two hours if the baby wants it, find it annoying and discouraging to hear others say, "You're not feeding him again, are you?" Older relatives and friends frequently lack understanding. Even professionals may be discouraging. All this means many mothers are discouraged needlessly from breast-feeding in the early weeks.

Support groups such as La Leche League can be extremely helpful. The International Lactation Consultant Association (ILCA) can direct you to a certified lactation consultant in your area (see Useful Addresses) who can help you with any worries or problems.

If you do have problems, try to persevere. Aside from the physical advantages for the baby, breast-feeding offers a unique bond of closeness between mother and baby once initial problems are overcome:

"I can't imagine not having fed my baby myself. It was the most wonderful thing that, whenever I was exhausted or she was fretful, we could just sit down and relax and be totally absorbed in one another. It was so easy, so natural and immediately made me feel at peace with myself and the baby . . . even at 4 a.m., it was easy just to pick her up and latch her on. Sometimes I would doze back to sleep. It was a wonderful feeling as she grew to think that I had done it all myself."

⌐ The postnatal checkup

Six weeks after the birth you will return to the hospital or your doctor's office for a checkup to ensure that your body is returning to normal after the birth. The doctor will feel your abdomen to check that the uterus has returned to its normal size. Your blood pressure and weight will be noted. You will be asked if you have had any unusual bleeding, pain or discomfort. (It is quite common for the lochia—the blood loss after the birth—to continue for more than six weeks. Some women have already had a period by this time.) Any scars from tears or episiotomies will be checked. Your breasts and nipples may be examined if you have problems with breast-feeding.

You may also discuss contraception with your doctor if this has not already been arranged. Women who use a diaphragm will usually have it refitted at the postnatal check. Everything may not have returned to its normal shape and size by this time, so it may need checking again a few weeks later. An IUD can also be refitted at six weeks. It isn't usually done right after the birth because the uterus is still contracting and may expel the device. If you want to take the Pill, the usual combined estrogen/progestogen pill is not suitable if you are breast-feeding because it affects the milk supply. The mini-pill or progestogen-only pill can be taken within seven days of the birth. Some mothers do not like the idea of taking any drug while breast-feeding, however. Small quantities of hormones do get through to the baby, but there is no evidence to date that this is harmful. Many couples rely on the condom as a temporary measure because it really is an ideal method at this time.

You will have the opportunity to raise any worries you have about your own health or that of the baby, including problems with breast-feeding. You may want to discuss problems you have with sex, especially if you have attempted intercourse and found it painful. It is very common not to have had sexual intercourse till after this postnatal stage. In fact, many women find they need the reassurance of the postnatal check that all is well before they do so.

If you did not have a Pap smear taken earlier in pregnancy, now is a good time to have it done.

6

Adjusting to Parenthood

The transition to parenthood is one of the greatest changes anyone can experience, yet most parents are caught unprepared. Often the pregnant woman and her partner focus on the birth itself as the "end of pregnancy" rather than on the continuation of caring for the baby. While prenatal classes may foster this problem, many childbirth-education teachers say they find some pregnant women just cannot see beyond the birth. They know they're going to have a baby, but they just can't visualize it or imagine what it's like.

✑ The early days

You've finally *had* the long-expected baby. Labor is over, whether it went well or badly, and you are holding a baby in your arms. What do you feel? Overwhelming love for this new person? Elation, joy, relief? Shock and disbelief: "Is this baby really mine? How will I cope?" Or doubt and fear: "Can I cope? Do I want this baby?"

Most new mothers probably feel a mixture of all these, but we are only supposed to acknowledge the first. To begin with, many women feel a sense of elation that they have given birth, especially if the labor has gone well. They may feel a real "high," showing off the baby to everyone, making lots of telephone calls to tell everyone the good news. After this "high" may come a feeling of exhaustion, of sudden flatness, weepiness and confusion; the classic "four-day blues." This may also be caused by hormonal changes as the level of pregnancy hormones drops and the mother's milk comes in.

Mothers may experience very strong physical reactions after labor. "It was a long labor, and I was completely exhausted," recalls Jamie, who had her first baby at 35. "I remember lying in the hospital bed and being afraid I couldn't breathe." Gina found she trembled uncontrollably for hours after the delivery. New mothers often have stitches, are stiff from the exertions of labor and perhaps squatting or crouching for long periods, have tender tummies and sore breasts, and lack sleep.

Paulette says, "I expected everything to be different, but I couldn't have imagined *how* different. After I spent those two days in the hospital, my partner drove me home with the new baby. I was driving through Phoenix and everything looked clearer and sharper than ever before, as if I were seeing it differently, almost as if I were on drugs or something."

Some mothers experience a profound feeling of unease, directed at the baby: Will he be all right? Will he go on breathing? Together with this is fear about whether the baby will thrive. Breast-feeding often causes a great deal of anxiety: Is the baby still hungry? Is there enough milk? Are my breasts and nipples the right shape? How often should I feed?

"I expected everything to be different, but I couldn't have imagined HOW different."

Many mothers remember the first few days at home with a new baby as a strange, timeless period, in which the mother spends a lot of time in bed and in the tasks of holding, changing and feeding the baby. Often the new mother has some help for the first week or so; the partner has time off work, a mother or mother-in-law comes to help.

If the labor has been long, difficult and did not end as the mother hoped (perhaps with a Cesarean section), the mother may initially feel depressed and have strong feelings of failure, which may color her initial reaction to the baby and to motherhood. A difficult labor, in which the mother feels control has been taken away from her and in which frightening and unpleasant procedures are carried out, can be upsetting, especially because the mother may fear something will go wrong for her baby.

No sooner has labor ended than the new mother is plunged into the relentless task of caring for her baby, day and night. Willa, a first-time mother at 36, says, "The hardest part is getting used to being useless at something again. At this age, you're used to being good at what you do—at your job, socially, running a home—when suddenly this baby comes along and you don't have a clue how to look after it. If I were 24, I would take learning something so new in stride better."

Another older mother recalls her feelings of horror when she realized what lay in store: "I remember thinking 24 hours after he was born, 'What have I done?'" One older mother remembers putting her baby down in its Moses basket in the center of the room and then sitting down and crying. "What was I going to do with him? I would have to wake up two or three times a night every night from now on. I could never go anywhere without him, or if I did, I would have to rush back home again, and I would worry about him all the time anyway. Nothing was ever going to be the same again."

Other mothers, despite the usual anxieties and stresses of adjusting to the new baby, recall the few weeks after the baby's birth as a very special, intense, thrilling time in their lives. "I felt so pleased with myself," says Robin, 38. "I had produced this perfect baby, and she seemed to thrive in my care. I loved the fact that she depended on me totally, I felt really important to someone for the first time in my life. There wasn't anything I'd rather do."

ᔆ Settling down

After the initial "honeymoon" period, where the mother usually has help and the admiration of friends and family, life goes back to "normal"—except it is nothing like the life the mother used to lead. For some, this is positive, but others—possibly the majority—feel much more ambivalence. Many first-time older mothers describe the birth of their first child as as "opening a whole new chapter" in their lives:

"You can't be alone. I miss my freedom, I miss the privacy," says one mother who is on her own with the baby, often all day long. Her whole time is taken up with the routine tasks of feeding, changing and pacifying the baby. When the baby sleeps, she uses the opportunity either to tidy up the home or to grab a short period of much-needed sleep to make up for the deprivations of the night.

"I feel like a zombie. Noon comes, and I still haven't gotten dressed. I'm too tired to do anything. I can't cope with the housework. I just don't care about it and I don't want to do it, but if the place got to be a mess I'd just feel too depressed."

Bonnie had twins at the age of 38. "My husband came home once and read me the riot act because I hadn't watered the houseplants, which were wilting. I had to go to a meeting and he took the afternoon off to look after the twins. When I came back I asked him if *he'd* had time to water the plants. He had to admit he hadn't. I think that one afternoon showed him a little bit of what I was going through."

Older mothers who have waited a long time to have a baby, especially those who have had fertility problems, may be horrified to find that once they have had the baby they do not feel overjoyed. "I did at first—for a few days. Then this sort of depression set in. I was so tired, I couldn't cope, I didn't feel much towards this baby. He was just a red-faced little thing who cried a lot. I

Life goes back to "normal"—except it is nothing like the life the mother used to lead.

couldn't bear to admit to myself this wasn't wonderful. How could I have gone through three years of infertility treatment, IVF and a miscarriage so I could be a mother, and then discover I didn't like it?"

This mother only found her equilibrium six months later, once she returned to work part-time.

"The thing about becoming a mother is that you instantly become a nonperson. You are 'just' a stay-at-home mom with a baby and you don't feel you count somehow." Claire, 39, a microbiologist, stands in her untidy kitchen with an 18-month-old clinging to her leg. She wears an old sweatshirt covered in marks left by grubby fingers, no make-up and hasn't combed her hair. She says, "I feel about as sexy and as intelligent as a potato. My husband changed jobs and I gave up mine, because we were moving and had a baby. I spend all day at home with this horrible toddler whining at me and getting into everything. I was a highly qualified and respected person at work, and now look at me! When the Chinese communists made intellectuals work on the land and do all kinds of menial tasks, Amnesty International said it was an abuse of human rights. Well, why isn't it an abuse of human rights when a highly qualified microbiologist has to wipe spit-up baby food off the kitchen floor and read *Pat the Bunny* all day long?"

After 40, the amount of time spent in deep sleep decreases. There are more awakenings at night and sleep itself becomes lighter.

⤸ Very, very tired

Exhaustion is one of the main complaints of older parents, who simply do not have the resilience of a young person. Linda, 40, a former magazine editor, said, "I do not think women in their forties realize the physical toll. I felt absolutely exhausted." One woman, who had sons at the age of 42 and 45, said, "I can't pretend there haven't been times when I've cried from one end of the weekend to the other out of sheer exhaustion."

Some recent research has shown that older men and women are less able to cope with sleep deprivation and disruption than younger people. After the age of 40 in particular, the amount of time spent in deep sleep decreases. There are more awakenings at night and sleep itself becomes lighter. As people get older they tend to lose the ability to fall asleep quickly, to sleep during the day or to sleep late to make up for a late or broken night.

As people age, it may be that sleep rhythms get more fixed and it becomes more difficult to adjust the pattern. After years of regularly waking and getting up at six, it may be harder for people to "sleep in." A new baby's pattern of sleeping for short periods may create havoc for the older mother's sleep patterns.

⤸ Finding help

Some older mothers, anxious to avoid the double burden of loneliness and exhaustion, use a mother's helper in the early weeks. Some hire a nanny or maternity nurse to help with the baby. This can be a good idea. It can give the mother help and companionship at a difficult time, but not always. Betsy found the maternity nurse undermined her own confidence and wanted to do things her way:

"It was my first baby and about the fiftieth she'd looked after. I felt helpless in comparison. Also, she didn't understand that I wanted to breast-feed the baby on demand. She kept saying he was feeding too frequently. She kept asking if she could give him a bottle so I could rest. She was obviously frustrated that she couldn't feed him. She fussed around and I couldn't relax. The only helpful thing was when she took the baby for a walk. In the end I let her go and hired a cleaning lady instead; that was much more useful."

✑ The crisis of motherhood

Sometimes late motherhood produces a real sense of crisis. Women's fantasies and expectations are not always met by motherhood and they can be confused when they are not able to manage the transition better. "Before he was born I had the illusion that I would continue my life like before—going out with friends to movies or concerts, just getting a baby-sitter when I needed one. I had no idea I would be so tired or the baby would make such demands that independence became impossible. I thought a baby wouldn't tie me down, and now look at me."

In an essay entitled "Psychotherapy with Pregnant Women," therapist Joan Raphael-Leff observes that women who come to motherhood later may have consciously set aside, avoided or denied pregnancy in past years. The conflicting emotions from these earlier years will still be in the subconscious. When they have the baby, these may resurface, causing conflict.

Older mothers are more likely than younger ones to have reached a point where their lives are ordered and they have things running much as they want. A baby's arrival can upset these routines and create chaos the mother cannot cope with. The transition from being an autonomous person to someone who is constantly at the receiving end of demands from the infant can be overwhelming. And the problem is, it's inescapable. "People kept saying to me, 'Why don't you go out and leave the baby for an afternoon or evening?' But that was just the point. I didn't want to leave her; I couldn't bear to be separated from her for a second. It was the tyranny of my own emotions I couldn't escape from, not her."

The birth of a second baby can present almost more problems than the first. Statistics show the trend to late motherhood has also shortened the space between births. If the older mother wants to have more than one child she has to squeeze them in quickly. Two surveys, done in 1988 and 1989, show that women who began childbearing in their 30s had an average of 27 months between their first and second baby and 30 months between second and third, compared with 30 and 35 for mothers in their twenties. The older the mother, the shorter the gap is likely to be.

The arrival of the second baby means the mother is now much more tied down than she was before. It was possible for her—alone or with her partner—to go out for the evening with the first baby in a backpack. But it is almost impossible to do anything spontaneously with a small baby and demanding toddler.

"My day was totally circumscribed," says Annie, whose children were born when she was 40 and 42. "I had to stick to my daily routine or it was hell. There was just under 18 months between them. James needed a nap for an hour after lunch or he was unbearable. He needed to be fed at regular times. Everywhere I went I had to take the baby in a sling and the toddler in a stroller, jars of puréed foods, drinks and all that stuff. For nearly a year I had two sets of diapers. By the time the baby was three months old I was so exhausted

*S*tatistics show the trend to late motherhood has also shortened the space between births . . . The older the mother, the shorter the gap is likely to be.

I didn't know what I was doing, and I was so bored I thought I would go crazy. If one of them was ill or it rained hard, I just didn't know how I would get through the day."

There is only one way to survive: with the companionship of

other mothers. Just someone to talk to, to say how you are feeling, can make all the difference. Unfortunately, older mothers may find it more difficult to meet other mothers in their situation. "I think there are more older mothers now, but when I had my son ten years ago there weren't so many around," says Vivienne, who was 41 when her daughter Ruth was born. "Most of the other mothers I met at prenatal classes were ten years younger and they thought they were 'old' to have a baby at 32! At first we would meet for coffee, but we didn't really have that much in common. I did want to meet other mothers like myself."

Other mothers had a different experience:

"I didn't think it was so unusual to have babies late. Most of the mothers in my prenatal class were in their thirties and some were in their late thirties. There were quite a few late mothers at the local playgroups, and I found a lot of support. We were all willing to help each other."

⤸ Effect on the couple's relationship

The longer a couple has been together before having a baby, the harder it may be to adjust to having a new baby. Research shows that the most stressful and difficult time in a marriage is after the birth of the first baby. There's no doubt that the birth of a baby can rock a marriage. The couple suddenly have much less time for one another and sex often suffers.

Having a baby can completely change the nature of a couple's relationship. "Before we had the baby we used to go out a lot, see friends, we were always doing something. Suddenly we were both at home, and our worlds completely diverged. He was still out there, doing things, meeting people, and when he came home all I had to report on was whether the baby had been particularly fretful or some possible problem with his health."

Sex, too, suffers in the weeks and often months after the birth. Studies have shown that the majority of mothers do not have sexual intercourse with their partners till at least six weeks after the birth of the baby. One study showed that more than half the women said they were less interested in sex three months after the birth than before pregnancy, and by a year after the birth 57% of women were still not having sex as often as before.

The delay in resuming sex after the birth is partly for medical reasons. Stitches have to heal, bruising has to clear up, there is a possible risk of infection, and the mother often still has lochia, or post-childbirth bleeding. Contraception, too, is an issue. A cap or IUD (intrauterine device) cannot be fitted until six weeks after the birth. The Pill is not advised because it may reduce the milk supply, and hormones are passed through in the breast milk to the baby. (The mini-pill does not affect the milk supply and there is no evidence the hormones harm the baby. However, the mini-pill has not been in use long enough for a generation to grow up and have children themselves, so most mothers are wary of taking this version of the Pill while breast-feeding.) Many women—and their partners—see the six-week check as an "all clear" to resume sexual relations if all is well.

Most mothers, however, find that their libido is altered by becoming a mother and that they do not want to have sex as often as before or even at all. This may be partly physiological, a result of the hormone changes following pregnancy and during breast-feeding. It may be partly psychological, and it may also be partly due to exhaustion.

Breast-feeding in particular seems to have an effect on libido. While nursing her baby, the mother has a high level of a hormone, prolactin, in her body, which helps suppress ovulation. This seems to dampen libido and may also lead to a decrease in vaginal lubrication. This may be nature's way of making sure the mother doesn't get pregnant again too soon and that the baby isn't therefore displaced from the breast. In hunter-gatherer societies, the oldest kind of social group, it is typical for the baby to be weaned from the breast when the mother conceives again. This isn't usually until the first child is three or four years old, partly because frequent breast-feeding acts as a contraceptive, but also because sexual intercourse is taboo when the mother is nursing a young baby. In such cultures breast milk is an important source of protein for the young child. In some regions of Africa, the word for some kinds of malnutrition means "baby displaced too soon from the breast."

Some mothers say sex and breast-feeding don't mix: "I would have this tiny, delicate baby at my breast, stroking me with his little hand, and then I'd put him down and this big hairy male hand would grab me." Some women find they do not like having their breasts touched by their partner while breast-feeding: "I felt my breasts were for my baby. If my husband touched them they'd start leaking milk and, because I wasn't the world's greatest milk producer, I'd worry about the milk that was going to waste. I also used to leak milk when I had an orgasm, so we always had have to have sex just after I'd fed the baby."

Other mothers find they enjoy the physicality of breast-feeding and enjoy sharing it with their partner: "I had plenty of milk—too much, in fact—so sometimes I'd let Nick have a taste. It was also useful sometimes—I'd get him to suck a little to get the milk to let down when I wanted to express some, or if I got overfull and engorged."

Psychological reasons why the mother may not want sex have to do with her image of her body and of motherhood. This may especially be the case if a mother has had a bad labor. "I felt as if I had been raped. I had been taken over, manhandled by doctors, and awful things had been done to the most intimate parts of my body. Aside from all the stitches, inside and out, which got infected and took weeks to heal, I felt traumatized. I couldn't bear to be touched for months afterwards."

Others feel they have lost some of their sexual attractiveness. This may be more true of older mothers, who may find that the stresses of pregnancy and birth take a heavier toll on their body and that it takes longer to get fit again. "I had put on weight and my tummy was just a flabby, empty bag. My breasts had changed shape and I just didn't feel that I could be attractive to my husband."

Again, other mothers, especially those who have enjoyed a good birth experience, find the opposite. "I felt I was really a woman now—my breasts were large and full of milk. I went back to my original weight very soon after the birth, and I felt really sexy and fulfilled. Maybe that was also because my partner made it clear that he found me very exciting and sexy as a mother."

Many partners do not understand if the woman has lost

interest in sex. Many, especially if they have not had sex at all in the late months of pregnancy and in the weeks after the baby is born, do not see why, after a couple of months, their sex life should not get back to normal. This can certainly strain the relationship. The important thing is to talk about it and get it out in the open, rather than bottling up feelings.

Some mothers find that, although they may not feel like having sex at first, it is very important for their partner. So they make the effort:

"I never felt like making love, with a new baby and a demanding toddler on my hands all day. But every so often I would take a deep breath and just do it. And then I always thought, 'This is really nice—why don't we do it more often?'"

Partners need to be sympathetic, understanding and supportive at this time.

Some women find that the more they make love, the more they feel like making love, while the longer they abstain, the less they feel like having sex. In other women, not feeling like making love is a symptom of depression. It expresses a lack of positive feelings for themselves as a mother.

"It took months for me to realize that my lack of interest in sex was really a symptom of postnatal depression. I felt so uninteresting, so ugly and so low in self-esteem that I didn't understand why anyone would want to make love to me."

Partners need to be sympathetic, understanding and supportive at this time, and most are. But there are also some who, not finding sex inside the marriage, look for it elsewhere. If the infidelity is discovered, the wife can be shocked and feel betrayed, though many marriages survive an infidelity. Fear their husbands may go elsewhere if they don't provide at least a minimum of sex is one reason many women say they have sex after childbirth: "It wasn't for me. I could take it or leave it, and would have been happier to leave it. But I couldn't help feeling sorry for him, and I didn't want him to get so desperate he'd start looking elsewhere."

Perhaps the best solution is for husbands to be actively

involved in childcare, getting up in the night, and so on. Then they may also feel too exhausted to want sex.

⌒ Going back to work

Making the decision of whether or not to go back to work after having the baby can be an agonizing one. Whatever their intentions, some mothers eventually decide not to go back to work. Commonly, this happens when the mother's only option is to go back to full-time work, and the money involved is not critical.

"I hadn't expected to find motherhood so fulfilling," says Laura, who was 40 when her first child was born. "I feel very lucky that I didn't have to go back to my job. *This* is my full-time job, the most important one there is. It would be crazy for me to be paying someone else to do what really matters while I'm out there pushing around pieces of paper."

The financial equation can be important. "I worked out what going back to work was going to bring in after I'd paid for childcare, fares and lunches, and after I'd paid taxes. It wasn't worth it," says one mother who considered going back to teaching. "I decided to wait until the children were in school." Other families are not in such a fortunate position. Carol found that working part-time in a boutique, after childcare and other expenses were accounted for, brought in fifty dollars a week. Her husband had a low-income job and this money made all the difference. "People would say to me, 'Why do you do this? It isn't worth it for fifty dollars.' And I would say, 'Of course it's worth it. With that fifty dollars I pay for the week's groceries.'"

Other women work because they cannot risk losing their job and they fear new opportunities won't be waiting for them in a few years' time. This is particularly true in times of high unemployment. "I knew the children would become more expensive. So, although we could afford for me *not* to work now, that might not be true in five years. I wasn't confident I would get a job after I'd been away for a few years. People would have forgotten who I was."

It's true: Women who choose not to work may find it isn't easy to get a job when they try to go back. "The women I knew who hadn't had children were in management positions. Now there were all these younger people coming in below me and at the level I'd been when I left. I realized they didn't want people with my age and experience in these jobs, they wanted youth. I realized it was going to be much more difficult to get back into work than I had originally thought."

∽ Child care

Finding adequate child care is also an important part of making the choice. "At first the idea of leaving her with anyone terrified me," recalls Georgianne. "Getting adequate child care was a nightmare. I got a list of the places licensed in my area, but when I went to visit the very first one I was discouraged. The woman had three other children and the home was in a depressing, stark apartment building. I just thought, no. In the end I paid a fortune for a series of nannies. They were all OK, but none of them stuck around much longer than six months."

Very few companies provide day care or nurseries. Local social-services departments have few day-care facilities, and these are mostly filled by single or special-needs mothers. Some churches and temples have day-care facilities, however. Private day-care services tend to be expensive, but they are becoming more common. Baby-sitters can be a good, inexpensive option if you find one you like. Nannies can live in if you have the space, or can come in for the day. Also, if you have one child and work part-time, you may be able to share a nanny with another mother to cut costs. If you work part time, au pairs can work out if you have the room. However, they aren't expected to work more than five hours a day. Also, they may be very young and inexperienced with small children.

Finding suitable child-care arrangements is often an ongoing worry for the working mother. What works when you have one baby will not be perfect when you have two preschool children. Often child-care problems get even more complicated when children start school: It's harder to find someone who wants to work for only two or three hours after school or during school vacations. And what do you do when your child is ill? Having both children and a job usually means:

◆ You have a reasonably understanding relationship with your employer.

◆ You are prepared to sacrifice some paid vacation days at those times when your child or baby-sitter is ill.

◆ Your partner is prepared to make some of these sacrifices, too.

Otherwise, the situation may become unworkable.

ᗧ Giving up work

Older mothers who have had fertility problems may be more likely than others to give up work for the baby. "They weren't very sympathetic about my taking maternity leave," says Pamela, "even though they acknowledged I had a right to it. They put me under a lot of pressure to come back early. I was breast-feeding, and I didn't want to stop. I thought, this is ridiculous. It's taken six years to have this baby; I'd better make the most of it. So I gave notice."

Not all women have a choice. Although it is against the law, some employers do use pregnancy as a reason to dismiss someone. "They did it in a sneaky way, restructuring the whole department, changing the job titles, but basically everything was the same except that I went," says Yvonne, who got pregnant at 38. "I didn't sue because I don't think I could have proved anything. And I did get some freelance work from them, which fit in with the baby. I wouldn't have gotten that if I'd taken them to court."

ᗧ Women who choose their career

A career is very important to some women. It's clear from the beginning that these women will take maternity leave and go back to work, full-time or sometimes part-time, if possible. Increasingly, perhaps because of feelings of nationwide economic instability or the fact that a second income may be vital for the family, women are going back to work sooner.

Recent maternity-leave legislation has made it easier for many women to combine a career and family. In the United States, you may take up to 12 weeks of unpaid leave, all at once or by reducing your hours at work (but you have to give 30 days' notice). Your partner may also have this option. You will retain your health benefits during this time, but you have to pay for them yourself. This legislation only applies if you work for a company with more than 50 employees and have worked at least 1,250 hours in the past 12 months. In Canada, the situation is much different. You may receive employment insurance benefits if you qualify. You must have worked at least 700 hours in the past 52 weeks. Most people will receive 55% of their normal incomes. You can take the benefits for up to 15 weeks, before or after the birth of your baby. To apply for benefits, contact your nearest Human Resource Centre of Canada (HRCC).

Despite such legislation, some women feel their career will be affected by having a child. Some organizations are very supportive of working mothers, but others, whether they admit it or not, will not promote a woman once she has a family. The unspoken reasoning is they believe she may be unreliable, taking time off work to be with sick children, or that she may not stay.

Some women find they have to work harder than ever to convince people their work hasn't suffered because they are parents. The kind of work they do is also important. "I had to give up my job as a publicist for a big company because I was expected not just to work nine to five. I had to be there in the evening whenever a story about us appeared in the press, attend conferences and meetings, and be available at all times to write a speech or statement. It wasn't possible to do this *and* see my child."

Some women who decide that career must come first make big sacrifices. At 43, with two young children, Judy decided to rent an apartment in downtown Atlanta. "I finally decided I would stay in an apartment in town during the week and go home on weekends. That way I could dedicate the week to my job and be available all the time, and I could give my weekends to the children. They were always in bed by the time I got home anyway, so they weren't really missing much. We had an excellent and experienced nanny and I don't think the children have suffered in any way."

Dolores made the same choice, working more than full time and spending only some weekends with her baby. It worked well until the baby was about nine months old, when he started crying and reaching out for his nanny every time Dolores picked him up. When he was a year old he still wouldn't go to her, so she gave up work and is now at home full-time with him and a second baby.

There are other ways around this problem. One older mother and her husband bought a house ten minutes away from the law practice where she worked. "It meant I could run home at lunchtimes for a quick breast-feed and spend half an hour with the children," she says. "Sometimes I would come home for an hour or so in the evening to bathe them and read a story and then zip back to the office for another few hours of work."

Older women may feel they can't take a few years off when they have a family, because they won't have the time or energy to climb up the ladder again afterward. Those who do opt to put family first may regret it. Mary, 38, with one son and then twins, was offered a job with an independent film-production company, which she turned down. "The twins were still very little and I wanted to be with them." Now they are all at school. She is looking for work, but it isn't available. "Did I make a mistake? I don't know."

Sex roles and division of labor

One of the most consistent findings of transition-to-parenthood studies is that the division of labor becomes more traditional after the birth of the first child. It doesn't seem to matter if the couple used to split tasks 50-50 or if the new mother returns to a full-time job. Inevitably one partner feels put-upon; usually it's the mother. One study showed that in families where roles are reversed and father is at home while mother works full time, the mother still performs 49% of child-care tasks.

Part-time working mothers often suffer the most.

"I think it works out if you've figured out the roles

beforehand—he is Daddy and earns the money and you are Mommy and look after the baby. But we were both doctors, both working, and trying to do everything in not a very well-defined way. We wound up arguing a lot of the time. I would say, 'I've had a harder day than you, so it's your turn to change the diaper.' And he would say, 'Yes, but I spent more hours in the office and I went to the hospital twice last night. . . .' We were both so tired we were just trying to put as much as possible on the other person. As a result, we were always trying to trade things off against the other. But you can't. Do two diaper changes equal one getting up in the night? It just can't work that way."

Part-time working mothers often suffer the most. They are at home part of the time. In this time they are expected to do things like take the baby to the doctor, go for checkups themselves, do the shopping and washing, clean the house. If the baby is sick, *they* have to take time off to look after him, often making up the time later so they do not get in trouble at work. Couples find they have little room to maneuver in; if one partner is late, they call the other to go home and relieve the baby-sitter. Endless juggling to cover all the bases often leads to fights.

*W*omen who have been mothers before often make interesting comparisons between how they were as young mothers and how they are as older ones. "I feel I'm a much better parent now than I was then," says Hillary.

"You're never in the right place at the right time as a working mother." Lindsay had her son at 41 and went back to work with an independent production company full-time when her son was six months old. She stuck it out for six months. "I found a very experienced and reliable nanny, but that wasn't enough, in the end. Once she called just as I was going into a meeting to say my son's temperature was 103. Should she call the doctor, and did I want to come home? I had to sit through the meeting but I couldn't concentrate on a single word." Her son always seemed to be ill; in the end the guilt was intolerable.

Cathy went back to work at 45 when her children were 5 and 7. "The little one started school and I thought, that's it, back to work. It was a disaster! The very first day at my job, the school called to say the children hadn't been picked up. The au pair, who I thought was reliable, had gotten on a bus going the wrong way and was completely lost. I had to leave work and get them. The very next day, just before I had to take minutes at a big meeting, the school called to say my 7-year-old had fallen in the school playground and needed stitches in his head. So I had to leave again. I sat with him as his head was stitched and thought, 'I have to be here for them. The au pair isn't good enough.'"

⌐ Positive feelings

Despite the difficulties, most mothers still have a positive impression about the experience of older motherhood. Those women who have been mothers before and have a late child, often in another relationship, make interesting comparisons between how they were as young mothers and how they are as older ones. "I feel I'm a much better parent now than I was then," says Hillary. "Then I felt trapped. I wanted to get out, and I felt restricted. Now I can take things slowly. I don't expect to get a lot done. I know this baby will only be small for a short time, so I'm content to take things slowly and just take each day as it comes."

*B*abies born to women in their twenties and thirties were more likely to be described as "difficult" babies than were those born to women in their forties.

Some older second-time mothers feel they need less support: "I knew what I was doing, I guess, so I didn't get upset the way I did with my first child. I also didn't feel the need to get out all the time—I didn't want to go out to play groups all the time, I didn't want to have other mothers and children over for lunch. I could live without that." Others say their child-care approach is more relaxed: "I don't have such high standards now. I know it doesn't matter. Sometimes she has a bad day or develops some horrible habit and I just think, she'll grow out of it. With my first child, if she didn't eat her carrots my whole day was ruined."

Research into how older mothers react to motherhood has been carried out by Kate Windridge and Judy Berryman at Leicester University in England. They studied 346 mothers who had had their babies at 40 or later, 100 of whom were first-time mothers. Sixty-three percent of first-time older mothers thought they would be more tired than they might have felt having a baby in their twenties. But less than half the second-time mothers indicated this, including those who *had* been mothers in their twenties. One-third did mention sleep as a high priority when they had time without their child.

One finding was that babies born to women in their twenties and thirties were more likely to be described as "difficult" babies than were those born to women in their forties. First-time older mothers felt they had greater patience because of their age. The majority of women with previous children felt that they were more relaxed than they were with their firstborns.

Older mothers frequently stated that they were better prepared for the demands of a baby and that they didn't miss their old social lives.

The overwhelming response to motherhood was very positive. These older mothers frequently stated that they were better prepared for the demands of a baby and that they didn't miss their old social lives. More first-time mothers said they would like more time away from their baby and with their partners. More than 90% said they enjoyed the experience of being a mother.

Only a tiny percentage (2%) said having a baby had been a bad experience. However, most of these women reported that the responses of family and friends had been shock, horror and disgust, confirming many older mothers' view that our society is prejudiced against older parents.

Looking ahead

As the children get beyond the baby stage, new difficulties can appear.

"I think one problem for the older mother is that you hit your real mid-life crisis at the same time as motherhood, and this tends to intensify everything. If you are 25 when you have a baby, you can think you'll get into a career when they start school and so on, you have all your life before you. When you have your children, as I did, at 39 and 41, they start school when you're 45. What have you done with your life? Can you stand the strain of motherhood and work? Are you too old to get back into your career? In a few years you're coping with menopause, with a host of emotional reactions, and you've still got to be a mother meeting the demands of very young children."

"Having a baby late—and an older husband—meant I had to cope with a lot of problems all at once. I had to cope with finding the right school for my 5-year-old child, toddler tantrums, go to the hospital with my husband for investigations into his heart problem, and deal with the heavy bleeding that seemed to be a precursor of menopause."

"When I compare myself to my son's friends' parents who are younger, I don't see any difference in the children's attitudes toward us. It's normal for all children to think their parents are old, fuddy-duddy, out of touch."

Looking ahead to when children are older, the majority of mothers did not seem to anticipate any particular problems in being in their fifties when their children were teenagers. "I think talk about the 'generation gap' is a lot of nonsense," says Karen, who was 39 and 41 when her two sons were born; now she is in her fifties. "When I compare myself to my son's friends' parents who are younger, I don't see any difference in the children's attitudes toward us. It's normal for all children to think their parents are old, fuddy-duddy, out of touch. They love to say, 'Oh Mom, surely you've heard of x or y?' In fact, I think there's less of a generation gap than there was between my parents' generation and us. There seemed to be such a gulf between our parents, who were young during the war, and us, who were young during the sixties. That's not the case now. Today's kids are just as likely to be listening to sixties music as to nineties and we share some of the same heroes. That certainly wasn't true of my parents!"

Older mothers who have teenagers and young babies in the house may find the generation gap has another angle. "My teenage son wants to play his music, have friends over and be generally noisy just when the baby's finally settled and I need peace and quiet. And then there are times when he wants help with his homework and the baby is screaming and needs attention. So it's a complex juggling act. On the other hand, Joey can be wonderfully kind and attentive to the baby and sometimes he's a great help. He'll baby-sit for a little while or make me a cup of coffee when I'm dead on my feet."

Teenagers with young half-brothers and sisters often oscillate between rapt attention and delight, and disgust and utter boredom, depending on their mood. "I think the important thing is to divide attention fairly equally, to give the older ones their time and the young ones theirs, and not expect the whole family to revolve around the baby," says Sarah, with two teenagers from her first marriage and a toddler and baby from her second.

✐ The final word: Love

The overwhelming majority of older mothers do not regret what they've done. "Most people don't regret being born, and most people don't regret being a mother either," says one older mother with two young children. "Once they are there, you love them, and that's it. You sacrifice yourself, you do things you would never believe you were capable of for them, you would die for them. And you love them with a kind of love that's completely different from anything else you've ever known. On the other hand, if any of us knew what lay ahead, who among us would ever be a mother?"

FURTHER READING

You'll find a multitude of books available today on pregnancy, childbirth, parenting and related subjects, such as infertility. The resources in this section are just a sampling of all that is available. The list below may be of particular interest to older mothers. Some of the older books mentioned may be out of print, but you can always check for them at your local library.

◆ Breast-feeding

La Leche League. *The Womanly Art of Breast-feeding, Fifth Edition.* New York: Plume, 1991.

Mason, Diane, and Diane Ingersoll. *Breast-feeding and the Working Mother.* New York: St. Martin's Press, 1986.

Moody, Jane, with Jane Britten and Karen Hogg. *Breastfeeding Your Baby.* Tucson, Arizona: Fisher Books, 1997.

◆ Childbirth

Kitzinger, Sheila. *Your Baby, Your Way: Making Pregnancy Decisions and Birth Plans.* New York: Pantheon Books, 1987.

—*Pregnancy and Childbirth.* Penguin, 1986.

Nolan, Mary. *Your Childbirth Class.* Tucson, Arizona: Fisher Books, 1998.

Parsons, Betty. *Preparing for Childbirth.* Tucson, Arizona: Fisher Books, 1997.

◆ Depression

Kleiman, Karen R., and Valerie D. Raskin. *This Isn't What I Expected: Recognizing and Recovering from Depression and Anxiety after Childbirth.* Oakland, Calif.: Harbinger, 1994.

◆ Fertility Issues

Jansen, M.D., Robert. *Overcoming Infertility: A Compassionate Resource for Getting Pregnant.* (Freeman, 1997)

Moss, Ph.D., Robert. *Helping the Stork: The Choices and Challenges of Donor Insemination.* (Macmillan, 1997)

Robin, Peggy. *How to Be a Successful Fertility Patient.* (Quill, 1994)

Salzer, Linda P. *Surviving Infertility: A Complete Guide through the Emotional Crisis of Infertility.* (HarperPerennial, 1997)

Silber, M.D., Sherman. *How to Get Pregnant with the New Technology.* (Warner Books, 1991)

◆ Parenting

Bettelheim, Bruno. *A Good Enough Parent.* New York: Vintage, 1987.

Grad, Rae, et al. *The Father Book: Pregnancy and Beyond.* Washington, D.C.: Acropolis, 1981.

McGrail, Anna. *Your Newborn and You.* Tucson, Arizona: Fisher Books, 1997.

Stewart, Nancy. *Your Baby from Birth to 18 Months: The Complete Illustrated Guide.* Tucson, Arizona: Fisher Books, 1997.

Wilson, Teresa. *Your Baby and Your Work.* Tucson, Arizona: Fisher Books, 1997.

◆ Pregnancy

Curtis, Glade B. *Your Pregnancy After 30.* Tucson, Arizona: Fisher Books, 1997.

—*Your Pregnancy Questions and Answers.* Tucson, Arizona: Fisher Books, 1997.

Kitzinger, Sheila. *Birth Over Thirty-Five.* New York: Penguin, 1995.

Thorn, Gill. *Having Your Baby: The Complete Illustrated Guide.* Tucson, Arizona: Fisher Books, 1997.

◆ Pregnancy Problems

Kohn, Ingrid, and Perry-Lynn Moffit, with Isabelle A. Wilkins, MD. *Silent Sorrow: Pregnancy Loss.* New York: Delta, 1992.

Lothrop, Hannah. *Help, Comfort and Hope after Losing a Baby in Pregnancy or the First Year.* Tucson, Arizona: Fisher Books, 1997.

Rich, Laurie. *When Pregnancy Isn't Perfect.* Rhinebeck, NY: Larata Press, 1996.

Useful Addresses

For a written response, send a stamped, self-addressed envelope with your query.

◆ General Information

American Academy of Pediatrics
Division of Publications
141 Northwest Point Blvd.
Elk Grove Village, IL 60007
Tel: 847-228-5005

American College of Obstetricians and Gynecologists (ACOG)
P.O. Box 4500
Kearneysville, WV 25430
Tel: 800-762-2264

Child Care Aware
(for locating child-care resources)
Tel: 800-424-2246

Doulas of North America
(for information about doulas, who support the mother during labor and after birth)
1100 23rd Avenue East
Seattle, WA 98112
FAX: 206-325-0472

Family Service Canada
600-220 Laurier Ave.
West Ottawa, Ontario K1P 5Z9
Tel: 613-230-9960

Mayo Foundation for Medical Education and Research
Mayo Health Oasis
(http://www.mayohealth.org)

National Organization of Single Mothers
P.O. Box 68
Midland, NC 28107-0068
Tel: 704-888-KIDS

Sidelines
(for women experiencing difficult pregnancies)
Candace Hurley, executive director
Tel: 714-497-2265
Tracy Hogenboom
Tel: 909-563-6199

The Vanier Institute of the Family
120 Holland Avenue, Suite 300
Ottawa, Ontario K1Y 0X6
Tel: 613-722-4007

Wellnet: Health and Wellness Network
(The Canadian Internet Directory for Holistic Health)
(http://www.wellnet.ca/new.htm)

Women's Health Bureau Canada
Tel: 613-952-3496

The Women's Bureau Publications

(for summaries of state laws on family leave)

U.S. Department of Labor

Women's Bureau Clearing House

Box EX

200 Constitution Ave.

Washington, DC 20210

Tel: 800-827-5335

Women's Health Interactive

(http://www.womens-health.com)

◆ Adoption

AdoptioNetwork (United States)

(http://www.adoption.org)

International Adoption for Canadians

(http://www.interlog.com/~ladybug/home.htm)

◆ Breast-feeding Information

Best Start

3500 E. Fletcher Ave., Suite 519

Tampa, FL 33613

Tel: 800-277-4975

International Lactation Consultant Association (ILCA)

The ILCA will refer you to a certified breast-feeding consultant in your area.

200 N. Michagan Ave.

Suite 300

Chicago, IL 60601-3821

Tel: 312-541-1710

La Leche League International

1400 North Meacham Road

Schaumberg, IL 60173-4840

Tel: 800-LA-LECHE, or check local telephone directory

La Leche League Canada

18C Industrial Drive

P.O. Box 29

Chesterville, Ont. K0C 1H0

Tel: 613-448-1842

La Leche League Canada Français

Secretariat General de la LLL

C.P. 874 Ville St. Laurent

Quebec, H4L 4W3

Tel: 514-747-9127

Medela, Inc.

(The company sells equipment in support of breast-feeding and
provides information)

P.O. Box 660

McHenry, IL 60051

Tel: 800-TELL-YOU

National Maternal and Child Health Clearinghouse

2070 Chain Bridge Road, Suite 450

Vienna, VA 22182

Tel: 703-356-1964

◆ Cesareans

C/SEC

22 Forest Road

Framingham, MA 01701

Tel: 508-877-8266

International Cesarean Awareness Network
1304 Kingsdale Ave.
Redondo Beach, CA 90278
Tel: 310-542-6400

Public Citizen's Health Research
(for information on C-sections and VBAC; send stamped, self-addressed envelope to receive information)
1600 20th Street NW
Washington, DC 20009

◆ Depression, Stress and Abuse

American Association of Marriage and Family Therapy
1133 15th Street NW, Suite 300
Washington, DC 20005
Tel: 202-452-0109

Depression After Delivery
P.O. Box 1282
Morrisville, PA 19067
Tel: 800-944-4773 (answering machine only)

National Child Abuse Hotline
Tel: 800-4A-CHILD (800-422-4453)

Society for Children and Youth of B.C.
3644 Slocan Street
Vancouver, BC V5M 3E8
Tel: 604-433-4180

◆ Fertility Issues

Toronto Centre for Advanced Reproductive Technology
(http://www.tcartonline.com/services/programs.gestational.html)

Women's Health Interactive
(http://www.womens-health.com/inf_ctr/inf_ctr.html)

◆ Miscarriage, Loss of a Baby, Problem Pregnancy

Abiding Hearts, Inc.

(Support for parents continuing pregnancy after diagnosis of fatal
   or nonfatal birth defects)

c/o Maria LaFond Visscher

PO Box 5245

Bozeman, MT 59717

Tel: 406-285-4408

Fax: 406-557-7197

The Alliance of Genetic Support Groups

35 Wisconsin Circle, #440

Chevy Chase, MD 20815

Tel: 800-336-4363

Fax: 301-654-0171

e-mail: alliance@capaccess.org

Compassionate Friends

P.O. Box 3696

Oak Brook, IL 60522-3696

Tel: 630-990-0010

SHARE

(Help after the loss of a baby in pregnancy or in the first year of life)

International Headquarters

St. Joseph's Health Center

300 First Capitol Drive

St. Charles, MO 63301-2893

Tel: 314-947-6164 or 1-800-821-6819

Fax: 314-947-7486

Index

sex-linked diseases 78, 98
sexual intercourse 65-66, 73,
    118, 142, 150-154
sexually transmitted diseases
    25, 27, 39, 60
SHARE 96
"show" 105
sickle-cell anemia 78
single mothers 6-7, 14
sleep 146, 147
"small-for-dates" babies 123
smear tests 40, 54, 59, 142
smoking 29, 40, 41, 42-43, 73
speculum 19
sperm:
    antibodies to 20, 28
    artificial insemination 29
    effects of drugs on 41
    fertilization 18
    genes 76
    GIFT 32-33
    hormonal treatment 28-29
    improving sperm count 29
    infertility 18, 27, 28
    IVF 31-32
    motility 20
    prostaglandins 65, 118
    tests 20, 21-22
spermicides 40
spina bifida 52, 55, 78, 82-83,
    89, 96, 97
split-ejaculate technique 29
sports 56
statistics, late motherhood ix
stillbirth 42, 52, 127-130
stitches 115, 116
streptomycin 44
stress 23, 43, 73
suppositories, prostaglandin
    118
surfactant 125
surrogate motherhood 36-37

T
Tay Sachs disease 78
tears, perineum 116
teenagers 162-163
temperature charts 19-20
termination of pregnancy ix, 1,
    11, 12, 25, 95, 96, 97-98, 100
testicles 19, 27-28
testosterone 71
tests:
    prenatal 59-61, 75, 84-101
    infertility 19-22
    preconception 53-54
    pregnancy 58
"test tube babies." *See* IVF
tetracycline 44
threatened miscarriage 69
thrush 40, 54, 140
thyroid gland 71
tiredness 62, 63, 146, 147
toxemia 61
toxoplasmosis 53
trace elements 49
tranquilizers 44
travel sickness 46
triple-screen test 89-90
trisomy 18 82
tubal pregnancy 27
Turner's syndrome 77
twins 34, 61-62, 78, 88, 123
Tylenol 44

U
ultrasound scans 84, 85-88, 91
umbilical cord 107, 109
undescended testicles 27-28
urine tests 60-61
uterus. *See* womb

V
vaccination, rubella 39
vacuum extraction 120

More fine titles from Fisher Books

$12.95 pb • ISBN 1-55561-143-5
6.125 x 9.25, 384 pgs, b/w illustrations throughout,
20/carton, 36th printing

Your Pregnancy Week by Week
Third Edition
Glade B. Curtis, MD, OB/GYN

The most up-to-date book available for pregnant women, *Your Pregnancy Week by Week* is the top-selling pregnancy book written by a doctor.

Dr. Curtis designed its unique format to help all women from before they conceive their baby until they give birth. A delightful new feature offers a "tip of the week" to experienced mothers as well as women pregnant for the first time.

$12.95 pb • ISBN 1-55561-088-9
6.125 x 9.25, 384 pgs
Illustrated, 20/carton

Your Pregnancy After 30
Glade B. Curtis, MD, OB/GYN

The latest in this best-selling series—an important and timely resource for the rapidly growing number of women becoming pregnant after age 30. Covers: achieving pregnancy after 30, multiple births, managing fatigue, tests for baby and mother, nutrition and weight management and workplace safety.

$12.95 pb • ISBN 1-55561-122-2
6 x 9, 234 pgs, b/w illustrations, 20/carton
3rd printing

Breastfeeding Your Baby
A National Childbirth Trust Guide
Jane Moody, Jane Britten and Karen Hogg

Over 200 mothers describe what helps and what hinders the breastfeeding experience. Written by three breastfeeding counselors, this up-to-date book answers the variety of questions parents have about breastfeeding.

Reassuring, comprehensive advice.